Advance Praise for

Understanding the Lived Experiences of Autistic Adults

"Adam and Sneha have created a beautiful and very much-needed book. Reading this book brings me hope. While my lived experience is different than that of Adam, I see so many recurring themes in my own life and in the lives of the learners who I support. The combination of narrative and research is engaging and makes a convincing argument for qualitative, lived-experience research. This work is mirrored by current and emerging research on Community-Informed Practice and Neurodiversity Affirming Practice. It is my opinion that this book needs to be included as essential reading for any person, autistic and allistic, who interacts with autistics (which really is everyone). But this book should be included in the required reading for any person who provides support for autistics in any setting."

—Brian Middleton, M.Ed., IBA, BCBA, LBA,
The "Bearded Behaviorist," Autistic Advocate

"Mathur and Valerius provide an articulate view into the lived experiences of individuals diagnosed with autism spectrum disorder. As an ABA practitioner and scholar, it made me think deeply about how clinicians may go about the implementation of compassionate ABA services. This book is a timely and significant contribution relevant for anyone with that goal in mind."

—Adel C. Najdowski, Ph.D., BCBA-D, Program Director, MS Applied Behavior Analysis, Pepperdine University, Los Angeles, California

"Dr. Mathur and Mr. Valerius have crafted a critical and engaging book that amplifies the voices of autistics through vibrant qualitative research. As a psychologist, I found this to be enlightening, highly educational and a vital contribution to the literature as it addresses the lack of representation of autistic voices. It's an insightful and useful tool and an essential addition to any clinician's library. As a mother of an autistic child and consumer of ABA services, this encouraging book resonates with me on a personal level, and

I believe it is required reading for anyone who loves, works with and supports autistics, particularly if ABA is part of their journey."

—Madeeha Mir, Ph.D., Counseling Psychologist and Instructor,
New York University

Understanding the Lived Experiences of Autistic Adults

Disability Studies in Education

Susan L. Gabel and Scot Danforth
General Editors

Vol. 27

The Disability Studies in Education series is part of the Peter Lang Education list.
Every volume is peer reviewed and meets
the highest quality standards for content and production.

PETER LANG
New York • Berlin • Brussels • Lausanne • Oxford

Sneha Kohli Mathur and
Adam Paul Valerius

Understanding the Lived Experiences of Autistic Adults

PETER LANG
New York • Berlin • Brussels • Lausanne • Oxford

Library of Congress Cataloging-in-Publication Control Number: 2022054465

Bibliographic information published by **Die Deutsche Nationalbibliothek**.
Die Deutsche Nationalbibliothek lists this publication in the "Deutsche Nationalbibliografie"; detailed bibliographic data are available on the Internet at http://dnb.d-nb.de/.

ISSN 1548-7210
ISBN 978-1-4331-9919-6 (paperback)
ISBN 978-1-4331-9917-2 (ebook pdf)
ISBN 978-1-4331-9918-9 (epub)
DOI 10.3726/b20299

© 2023 Peter Lang Publishing, Inc., New York
80 Broad Street, 5th floor, New York, NY 10004
www.peterlang.com

All rights reserved.
Reprint or reproduction, even partially, in all forms such as microfilm, xerography, microfiche, microcard, and offset strictly prohibited.

Contents

List of Tables   ix
List of Figure   xi
List of Abbreviations   xiii
Acknowledgments   xv

I. Introduction to Literature, Theoretical Framework, and Methodology
1. Introduction   3
   Background 4
   Adulthood and Autism 6
   Literature Review 9
   Autobiographical Research 16
   Study Objectives 18
   Conclusion 21

2. Methodology and Theoretical Framework   23
Trustworthiness 25
Research Questions 29
Theoretical Framework: Social Model of Disability 29
Methodological Frameworks 33
Narrative Inquiry 33
Disability Life Writing 37
Data Collection 38
Data Analysis 40
Constant Comparison Model 48
Researcher Positionality 50
Conclusion 53

II. Redefining Experts: Adam's Story
3. Childhood Memories   57
4. Adolescence   63
5. Transitioning to Adulthood   73
   College Experiences 74
   Employment 78
   Living Alone 82
6. Life in Orange County, California   85
   Employment 89
   Friendships and Romantic Relationships 101
   Relationship With Parents 105
   Concluding Thoughts 106

III. What Does This Mean?
7. A Thematic Analysis of Adam's Story and Autobiographical Accounts   109
   Isolation 111
     Mental Health 117
     Societal Expectations 122

 Medical Treatment and Diagnosis 128
 Influence of Parents 130
 Differences in Needs: Examples From Education and Employment . . 136
  Examples From Education 138
  Examples From Employment 145
  Differences in Needs 149
 Empowerment 150
  Understanding One's Own Behaviors Through ASD Diagnosis . . . 156
 Relationships 165
  Friendships 166
  Romantic Relationships 170
  Parenting 173
 Conclusion 174

8. Findings   177
 Neurodiversity Paradigm 178
 Monotropism Theory 185

9. Discussion and Conclusion   193
 Research Questions and Interpretation of Findings 194
  Isolation (Mental Health, Societal Expectations, Medical Treatment and Diagnosis) 195
  Influence of Parents 196
  Differences in Needs: Examples From Education and Employment. 196
  Empowerment (Understanding Behavior via ASD Diagnosis, Sensory Experiences) 197
  Relationships (Friendships, Romantic Relationships, Parenting) . . . 197
 Recommendations From Autistic Authors 197
 So What? 208
  Researchers 209
  Teachers, Therapists, Psychologists, and Psychiatrists 209
  Parents and Families 210
  General Society 210
  Board Certified Behavior Analysts 211

Limitations of Study 212
Future Research 213
Significance of Study 214
Call to Action 215

References 217
About the Authors 225

List of Tables

Table 1. Academic Literature Search Results   10
Table 2. Neurodiversity Paradigm   184
Table 3. Monotropism Theory   190
Table 4. Demographic Information   199
Table 5. Advice from Autistics About Autism   204

List of Figure

Figure 1. NVivo Coding Word Cloud   43

List of Abbreviations

Abbreviation	Meaning
ABA	Applied Behavior Analysis
ACLU	American Civil Liberties Union
ADD	Attention Deficit Disorder
ADHD	Attention Deficit Hyperactivity Disorder
ASD	Autism Spectrum Disorder
AS	Asperger Syndrome
DoR	Department of Rehabilitation
DS	Disability Studies
DSM	Diagnostic and Statistical Manual of Mental Disorders
HCBDDS	Hamilton County Board of Developmental Disabilities Services
HFA	High Functioning Autism
ICC	Intensive Care Center
ICD-10	International Statistical Classification of Diseases
IEP	Individualized Education Plan
IRB	Internal Review Board
JVS	Jewish Vocational Services
MDC	My Day Counts
NAMI	National Alliance of Mental Illness
NOS	Not Otherwise Specified
NT	Neurotypical

Abbreviation	Meaning
PDD-NOS	Pervasive Developmental Disorder-Not Otherwise Specified
SBH	Severely Behaviorally Handicapped
TAG	Talented and Gifted

Acknowledgments

Sneha

My successes during my professional career thus far have, in large part, been due to support and encouragement of my family, friends, peers, and colleagues. To Adam, coauthor of this study, I am humbled you trusted me with your story and feel privileged to have learned from you and work alongside you. You are a resourceful and hardworking person, and the courage you have shown by sharing your story is inspirational.

To my professional and personal mentors and advisors, who helped shape my understanding of the academic world in so many ways, I thank you for helping me develop skills I need to better myself as a researcher and clinician: Dr. Scot Danforth, Dr. Lilia Monzo, Dr. Amy Jane Griffiths, Dr. Dawn Hunter, Dr. Jonathan Tarbox, Kristine Rodriguez, Dr. Cynthia Woelfel, Dr. Madeeha Mir, and Dr. Peter Gerhardt.

To my family, I would not be who I am or where I am without you. Mom and Dad, you have always encouraged me to follow my dreams, and when I tell you my new goals, your response is always, how can we help? You have set an example for me on how to work hard to achieve my dreams, to value and appreciate everything I have earned, and to also appreciate the journey. You have instilled in me a strong work ethic and, perhaps most importantly, you have taught me the importance of having work–life balance. To my sister, Sonali, you have dealt with more in the last year than many people have to deal with in a lifetime. I admire your strength, resilience, honesty, and commitment to working toward causes you believe in. Your work ethic is unparalleled and the passion you have toward creating an equitable future for today's youth is inspirational. Thank you for your continual love and support. Sister Code!

To my husband, Neil, I dream many dreams, but with you by my side I know those dreams can come true. Thank you for the sacrifices you've made so I can achieve my dreams, for encouraging me and pushing me to continue working when I wanted to give up, and, most of all, for never doubting I could achieve this milestone. To the cosmos and back. Finally, to my son, Rohan, amid a global pandemic, you had to share your mommy with writing this book and I am so proud of how you handled the many sudden transitions over the last 2 years. I am continually amazed by your humor, compassion, and desire to include everyone in your activities.

Seeing the world through your eyes is truly my life's greatest privilege. My hope for you is that you grow up in, and contribute to, an inclusive world that values everyone's differences.

Adam

The process of this book was overwhelming for me, many-a-time, because of the memories I had to recall to put together this work of art. I get told that I am an inspiration and I bring hope to mental health consumers, and autism parents. What I hope to achieve by sharing my story is to spread that same hope to a broader range of people who I may never meet face to face. When I tell some people what I'm doing with my life they admit they didn't think someone with this condition could do most of these things because the media stereotypes and portrayal of autism. I want to break the stereotypes. I am writing this book with Sneha, who to me represents an autism advocate. I want to educate people how difficult it actually is for someone with autism to be accepted in the neurotypical mainstream workplace and society. I feel more catharsis from legitimizing my story by writing a book rather than posting on social media where I usually get ignored or attacked. Sneha helped me put my story into words and I am proud of my story and my life.

To my parents: while I am starting off the story mentioning the date in my adolescence that we'd all agree was the absolute worst for us all, please don't miss the parts where I acknowledge that my relationships with each of you have healed more than I ever thought was possible. My expressions of gratitude for things you've done for me over the course of my life haven't always been that sincere, but my gratitude has been genuine regardless of how I expressed it in the past.

Part One

Introduction to Literature, Theoretical Framework, and Methodology

Chapter One

Introduction

Adam Paul Valerius

On December 10, 1999, I left my high school an hour early because I was being teased by the other students. I tried to go home, but I forgot my key, so I was locked out. My parents were home but did not let me in the house until I attempted to break the door down with a sledgehammer. Once they let me into the house, there was an hour-long shouting match, and then they called the police because they felt that I was a threat. I was no threat. If they had just opened the door when I rang the bell, I would never have grabbed the sledgehammer.

The police blocked the street, making me look like a terrorist. My dad wanted me arrested and sent to juvenile hall, and my mom wanted me hospitalized. My parents and the police argued for an hour and then the police decided to take me to the hospital. I was standing there, not a part of the conversation. Every time I tried to break into the conversation, I was shouted down. It was during this hospital stay that the psychiatrist at the hospital decided I needed long-term care at a facility called The Buckeye Ranch.

I was very angry that I was being taken to a place where I would be locked up. When I got there, I remember thinking it looked like a jail because there were bars around the buildings, and the small room felt like a jail cell. That ended up being my home for the next 94 days.

My name is Adam Paul Valerius, and this is my story (A. P. Valerius, personal communication, March 2018).

Background

The above passage is an excerpted conversation I had with Adam and touches on myriad issues Adam has had to face. These issues have included bullying from other students, lack of understanding about the experience of someone with Autism Spectrum Disorder (ASD), and a broken system of communication between an autistic person and his parents. Other challenges have involved struggles with law enforcement personnel, refusal to let Adam have autonomy in his own treatment and living arrangement, and overall frustration from choices made *for* him rather than *with* him. Desire to understand Adam's experiences, and how they have affected him, led us to delve into this research study.

I first met Adam in January 2016; I had been looking for an intern for my start-up company, Spectrum Success. The goal of Spectrum Success was to help autistic adults gain meaningful employment opportunities with competitive salaries. Adam emailed me and soon became the marketing intern for Spectrum Success. In turn, I helped Adam with his employment skills, and Adam now works full-time as a Lead Packager at General Tool. During the year Adam worked with me, I got to know him and gained new perspectives about ASD. After establishing a relationship of mutual respect, I had the privilege of getting to know Adam's experiences on a much deeper level as he shared in-depth stories about his past.

Many autistic adults have contacted me with similar stories. They have undertaken various therapies (e.g., applied behavior analysis, occupational therapy, speech therapy), either until graduating high school or the age of 22, which is when funding provided through school districts for most of these services end. At 22, on the cusp of adulthood and prior to some of the most daunting experiences of their lives, support systems are taken away from autistic adults.

This loss of services, combined with a lack of available adult support services when students reach either cutoff milestone, is referred to as the service cliff (Laxman et al., 2019). Such a void in services can only be remedied by conducting research to better understand experiences and desired supports of autistic adults. To provide adequate support services for these individuals, research methods must first align with their desires.

This study was a two-part process, with Internal Review Board (IRB) approval obtained August 2018. Part One of this study involved having conversations with Adam to explore how his experiences shaped his life as an autistic adult. Though I respect use of person-centered language, Adam requested I use identity-first language in my research to "reflect how he talks in real life." As he explained:

> It is easier when talking to use identity-first because it's fewer words. I was always so irritated listening to my long-winded case manager in Cincinnati that I strive not to be long-winded in how I talk to others since I don't want anyone else to talk to me the way she did. (A. P. Valerius, personal communication, November 22, 2020)

Although I have used person-centered language in the past, Adam encouraged me to use identity- first language because he believed "nonautistic people can talk about autism in identity-first language so that they sound more like autistic people talking about our condition. If everyone uses identity-first language like we do, the conversation is easier to follow and makes more sense" (A. P. Valerius, personal communication, November 22, 2020). Though Adam sometimes referred to autism as a disability, not every autistic person views autism as a disability. Jackson- Perry et al. (2020) helped clarify language used in this study, noting:

> References here and later to disability theorists are therefore *not* a statement of ontological positioning (that autism 'is' a disability, and that autistic people 'are' disabled), but an acknowledgement of two points. First, of the *usefulness* of some strands of disability theory in approaching autism, and second, of our opinion that autistic people and communities are subject to many tensions in common with disabled communities. (p. 126)

Part Two of this research included gathering data in the form of published autobiographies, memoirs, and first-person stories written by autistic individuals. Focus of analysis in this study was Adam's story, for which I used the grounded analysis element of grounded theory. I then used the constant comparison method when analyzing autobiographies written by other autistic individuals to "deliberately search for commonalities throughout the data and use an evolving repertoire of established code" (Saldaña, 2016, p. 79). The autobiographies served as both part of the literature review and data for analysis. Through the constant comparison process, I expanded on Adam's spoken experiences by discovering key patterns and insights about the autism community.

Instead of viewing a disorder or impairment as something to be "cured" or "fixed" by the age of 22, this study interpreted disability as a difference. Differences turn into a disability based on social, political, and cultural contexts (Baglieri et al., 2011; Siebers, 2011). Additionally, my research aimed to understand lived experiences, triumphs, and challenges of autistic people. I put their voices first to help emphasize how widespread differences are, with varying levels of support needed across individual lifespans. I stressed that deference to the notion of "disability" over "difference" simply serves to pathologize some of these differences. In this study, Adam was considered an expert on living with autism; for this reason, it was important to understand Adam's core values and beliefs in relation to the research topic. I asked Adam what adulthood meant to him, and his words defined "adulthood" in our research:

> Adulthood is freedom and independence, like you're finally in control of your own life instead of someone else controlling your life for you. Responsibilities come with the freedom and independence, but adulthood is being able to handle those responsibilities. Independence is like getting to see the doctor without your parents right there. Having a bank account that they don't have access to. Paying your own rent and bills. (A. P. Valerius, personal communication, March 15, 2018)

Adulthood and Autism

Research showed before the 1990s, adulthood outcomes for autistic individuals reflected patterns of social isolation and dependence on family members or sheltered communities (Levy & Perry, 2011). Gerhardt and Lainer (2010) argued to effect policy change for autistic adolescents and adults, funding first needs to go toward research to determine the most effective, encouraging, evidence-based, and socially valid supports for successful lives in society. For example, employment is often a source of financial independence and contributes to a person's quality of life; yet, for autistic adults, support services are minimal, which makes seeking employment a huge challenge (Gerhardt & Lainer, 2010). Further compounding the problem is once an autistic student turns 22, they typically no longer have legal rights to support services.

Instead, most adult support services have their own eligibility requirements with vastly different service costs (McDonough & Revell, 2010). Burden of responsibility often transfers to autistic adults, and occasionally their families, to navigate a confusing system with minimal services or guidance.

Adulthood is typically characterized by expected increases in responsibility and independence, which leads to decreasing family assistance amid a period of individual identity formation (McKenzie et al., 2017). With this new period in a young adult's life comes an increase in social, emotional, and organizational demands (Arnett, 2000). Elias and White (2018) noted these demands are often amplified for autistic adults, and there remains a void in literature addressing how best to provide necessary guidance during this critical time of transition. If not adequately assisted, autistic adults may experience lapses in their physical and mental health (Nicholas et al., 2017).

According to Gerhardt and Lainer (2011), literature related to outcomes for autistic adults often introduced themes of inadequate transition planning, lack of coordination between service providers, issues related to staff and service provider retention, and minimal evidence-based practices for adult support services. Relatedly, Nicholas et al. (2017) argued existing research on transitional needs for autistic adults has disproportionately focused on transitions to employment and higher education, leaving other issues, such as housing, social networks, and relationships, neglected. Interestingly, none of the issues described above are directly related to challenges of ASD. Rather, these issues indicate a lack of societal belief in potential for adults with ASD to find success as members of their communities and places of employment.

This limited understanding is precisely what needs to be addressed in future literature (Gerhardt & Lainer, 2011).

Although employers have begun recognizing value in autistic employees, community members and employers often do not know enough about ASD and necessary supports to create a successful work environment for them (Nicholas et al., 2017). Nicholas et al. reported service providers, college staff, and employers do not have access to research and empirical data outlining this information. To address this problem, this study was ultimately written (and will be published) as a book, rather than an academic article, allowing my findings to be accessed by a much larger audience. This study strove to understand and improve quality of life for autistic individuals, and it should be distributed to families and professionals to ease burdens of adulthood faced by autistic people (Gerhardt & Lainer, 2010). My findings should therefore be disseminated via mediums accessible to most of society, including books, social media, and blog posts. Publishing exclusively in academic journals does not allow for policy change to occur on widespread levels because most people cannot access these journals (Gerhardt & Lainer, 2010).

This study used narrative methodology through a social model of disability lens. I included voices of autistic adults to best understand their needs, aspirations, goals, challenges, and desires as they transitioned to adulthood. Disability studies (DS), which supports the social model of disability, recognizes having a disability to be a subjective experience and influenced by societal attitudes (Nadesan, 2005). The narrative component of this research allows readers to understand these subjective experiences directly from the source. To further delineate the significance of this study, it was important to review existing literature, which largely emphasized ASD as a medical deficit. In existing literature, use of first-person narrative structure to understand needs of people on the autism spectrum was rare.

Literature Review

Existing literature typically employed the medical model of disability to emphasize perceived deficits in skill acquisition that hinder many aspects of adulthood for adults diagnosed with ASD. Additionally, many articles related to autistic people transitioning to adulthood were often written by or about experiences of parents, siblings, or service providers, rather than directly by or about the autistic person. I narrowed my search to five databases typically used to locate autism-related material when searching for literature either written in first-person narratives of autistic people or related to adulthood transitional needs and experiences: Academic Search Premier, Education Full Text (H.W. Wilson), ERIC (EBSCO), ERIC (ProQuest), and PsycINFO. Due to lack of autism research related to adult experiences and needs, there was no limit of publication year in my search criteria. Though existing scholarly literature is reviewed in this section, additional research was gathered in the form of published autobiographies, memoirs, and first-person stories written by autistic people. Including these forms of research allowed for an additional layer of understanding and added substance to traditional literature. Finally, honing in on first-person perspectives honored a main tenet of DS: Charlton's (1998) book, *Nothing About Us Without Us*, was the first book to explore oppression disabled people faced, intertwining theory with interviews of first-person experiences. The title of their book has now become a rallying phrase for the disability rights movement, highlighting voices of people with disabilities as central to discussion of disability-related experiences and needs.

As Table 1 demonstrates, there were scarce search results for adulthood transition and ASD, even though ASD is a popular topic of research (with 78,503 search results); the largest search result for my research focus produced 356 hits. Though this paucity of related literature affirmed adulthood transitional needs for people with ASD had not been adequately researched, even fewer results emerged when I added first-person or lived experiences to ASD and adulthood search criteria. The decline from 78,503 search results to 356 specifically pertaining to ASD adulthood transitional needs reflected current practices and policies for adults with ASD. Existing services largely focus on early intervention, with goals of modifying and "fixing" behaviors once individuals reach adulthood. Furthermore, lack of inclusion via first-person narrative to understand lived experiences of autistic people reflected enduring dominance of the medical model, both in research and practice. This search result demonstrated to influence policy and practice, it is essential to first modify our research methodologies.

The first of two articles from my "Transition to Adulthood, Autism Spectrum Disorder + Narrative" keyword search focused on experiences of two adult women with ASD in relation to their sense of belonging, acceptance, support, and inclusion during transitional periods in their lives (Pesonen et al., 2015). The authors used semistructured interviews and document data to collect narrative accounts of participants' experiences and found emerging adulthood (ages 18– 25) was a critical period during which social supports were needed for autistic women to increase positive experiences related to sense of belonging. The second article used photovoice with 11 autistic adults (ages 18–23) to understand effective coping strategies for stressors associated with youth transition to adulthood (First et al., 2019). Photovoice referred to

Table 1. Academic Literature Search Results

Keywords in Search	Number of Search Results
Autism Spectrum Disorder	78,503
Transition to Adulthood, Autism Spectrum Disorder	356
Transition to Adulthood, Autism Spectrum Disorder + Narrative	2
Adult Autism Experiences + Narrative	137
Adult Transitional Experiences + Autism Spectrum Disorder	33
Adult Transitional Experiences + Autism Spectrum Disorder + First Person Narrative	0
Autism Spectrum Disorder + Lived Experiences	257
Autism Spectrum Disorder + Adult Transition + Lived Experiences	3
Autism Spectrum Disorder + First Person Narrative	32
Autism Spectrum Disorder and Adulthood + First Person Narrative	1

a narrative method in which participants were given cameras so they could photograph daily experiences—in this case, with an emphasis on stressors and coping methods—and share their lives in a nontraditional way. The authors also employed a phenomenological analysis of 11 young adults' narrative photographs and found the following supports helped them deal with adult transitional stressors: books, music, physical exercise, seeking support, spirituality, and building self-esteem and confidence by generating positive thoughts to counter bullying and stigma.

Only one of three articles located by my "Autism Spectrum Disorder + Adult Transition + Lived Experiences" search actually met the criteria. The first article considered experiences of siblings to autistic adults. The second article was not specific to autistic adults, but instead targeted those with pervasive developmental disorders who had history of aggressive behavior and psychiatric impairments. The third result was a dissertation; Jones (2017) interviewed eight men transitioning from high school to college in Texas with the goal of understanding social transition needs of young autistic adults. By acknowledging the lived experiences of these individuals, Jones was able to recognize self-determination skills, social media use, and participation in college orientation activities were related to increasing positive social outcomes as young autistic adults transitioned to college.

The search results for "Autism Spectrum Disorder and Adulthood + First-Person Narrative" produced the most thorough research article found in this review. In the article, DePape and Lindsay (2016) searched 10 electronic databases and found 33 articles related to lived experiences of autistic individuals. Of these articles, 15 focused on autistic adults. After conducting their research, they found first-person accounts were clearly underrepresented in literature and most "lived experiences" were told via parents, siblings, or healthcare provider accounts. When analyzing content in those 33 relevant articles, DePape and Lindsay discovered the following four themes: perception of self, interactions with others, experiences at school, and factors related to employment. Researchers can use these insights in future research, given the themes reflected needs coming directly from individuals we seek to support. Planning and implementation of care should include voices of autistic people as experts in their own experiences and needs. Weinstein (2001, as cited in DePape & Lindsay, 2016) stated autistic adults themselves echoed this need:

> With respect to experts in the field, some individuals with ASD were dissatisfied over being seen as secondary to their own disorder. Particularly, in the case of adults with ASD, they spoke about wanting to be seen as experts. This experience is consistent with the traditional medical model where doctors are gatekeepers of knowledge and patients are passive to the care they receive. (p. 68)

The majority of existing research interpreted actions of autistic people through the construct of their ASD diagnosis, which perpetuates stereotypes associated with autism. In contrast, the research articles described above used first-person perspectives to offer a different lens, humanizing experiences of autistic people rather than diagnosing them (DePape & Lindsay, 2016; First et al., 2019; Jones, 2017; Pesonen et al., 2015). Pesonen et al. (2015) focused on how society can provide social supports to help autistic people achieve sense of belonging, rather than placing burden on autistic people to modify behaviors in search of belonging. Furthermore, their research used open-ended interview questioning to explore themes of transitional experiences and support at different time periods in participants' lives (childhood, adolescence, and adulthood). This approach was undertaken in lieu of creating questions focused solely on understanding autism diagnosis. Additionally, use of photovoice by First et al. (2019) was an innovative way to ensure participants' voices were not only central to understanding their experiences, but actually allowed participants to direct the research. Jones (2017) also discovered social media was an important factor in building self-determination skills, taking into account unique needs of adults in the 21st century.

Finally, in the literature review conducted by DePape and Lindsay (2016), four themes emerged from first-person narratives: perception of self, interactions with others, experiences at schools, and factors related to employment. These findings were noteworthy when contrasted against Diagnostic and Statistical Manual of Mental Health (DSM-5) autism criteria, which included persistent deficits in social communication and social interaction across multiple contexts. Under this standard, criteria manifest through deficits in social–emotional reciprocity, deficits in nonverbal communicative behaviors used for social interactions, and deficits in developing, maintaining, and understanding relationships. Severity has been based on social communication impairments and restricted, repetitive patterns of behavior (American Psychiatric Association, 2013).

The majority of studies I located focused on medical and therapeutic supports to counter challenging behaviors described in DSM-5, which has long influenced provision of services. By analyzing first-person lived experiences of autistic people, DePape and Lindsay (2016) successfully identified new areas of further research and incorporated suggestions for new services for individuals. In their research, autistic adults held authority over their own needs and services, rather than researchers and medical professionals.

In Part One of my research, Adam and I expanded on the handful of studies directly addressing lived experiences of autistic adults. Speaking directly to individuals with autism and understanding their experiences, challenges, successes, and adjustments as they transition to adulthood is crucial, and it is vital to include their voices when designing programs, services, supports, and policies for adults on the spectrum (DePape & Lindsay, 2016; First et al., 2019; Grypdonck, 2006; Pesonen et al., 2015). For this reason, I spent a great amount of time speaking with Adam to understand his experiences and coconstruct his story. I also integrated his story with detailed experiences from published autobiographies and memoirs written by other individuals on the spectrum.

People with disabilities are often not interviewed directly because they are not taken as seriously as their nondisabled peers. This omission reflects a misguided societal hierarchy and leads to bias against people with disabilities (Kirby et al., 2015). Ignoring voices of autistic individuals does not enable society to understand what autistic people actually endure on a daily basis, nor does it allow for appreciation of what autistic people contribute to society (Hurlbutt & Chalmers, 2002). Using a first-person perspective in research allows autistic adults to broaden interpretation of academic findings and contribute to enhancement of quality clinical services (Angulo-Jimenez & DeThorne, 2019). Congruent with other research studies using first-person perspectives, Hurlbutt and Chalmers (2002) found autistic adults expected to be considered experts in the field of autism. They also found autistic adults wanted to be consulted on related issues and personally educate society about autism. After all, only someone with autism can truly know and understand what autism is (Angulo-Jimenez & DeThorne, 2019). Due to the void in research articles pertaining to adulthood experiences and autism, the following literature was found in noneducation-specific databases, but rather, psychology-specific databases, to broaden scope of this study.

Angulo-Jimenez and DeThorne (2019) argued there are varying views on autism in the autism community, and it is important for researchers to acknowledge these different views.

Using a first-person perspective allows researchers to recognize how autistic people understand and discuss their own experiences with autism. If our goal as researchers and clinicians is to help our clients, we should use the same language they use, rather than discussing autism solely through jargon. For example, "symptoms of autism" reflects a deficit model, whereas "experiences associated with autism" is more descriptive and neutral.

Angulo-Jimenez and DeThorne (2019) examined YouTube videos created and posted by autistic adults. When analyzing published first-person narratives, whether in the form of YouTube videos or in the case of my studied autobiographies, researchers benefit from consuming experiential accounts by autistic people and avoiding influence from other researchers. This objectivity makes quality of these data more authentic. For example, by using insights gained from published YouTube videos, Angulo-Jimenez and DeThorne found autism is a complex phenomenon when described by autistic people. This complexity is far different from typical interpretations of autism in the majority of existing literature, which tended to address autism using contexts of narrow and specific diagnostic criteria. Although there are arguably some benefits to diagnostic criteria, particularly when accessing and creating guides for treatment and support, incorporating first-person perspectives via YouTube videos allowed for a more complete understanding of the autistic individual experience.

In a study conducted by Kirby et al. (2015), autistic children were interviewed and described their experiences in terms of likes and dislikes, just as their neurotypical peers would. This similarity is significant because literature has typically described autistic peoples' experiences in terms of their diagnosis and limitations, rather than portraying them as humans worth understanding. Just as Angulo-Jimenez and DeThorne's (2019) analysis of YouTube videos showed, autistic people felt autism could best be understood as a difference rather than a disorder. Furthermore, in Kirby et al.'s (2015) research, some children emphasized in their responses desire to do things "like other people do" or "normalize" their behaviors (p. 320). This reflected longing to be understood in the same way as their neurotypical peers instead of in the construct of a diagnosis. When asked about their experiences, many children also used stories to detail specific examples, which added depth to their interviews and helped guide researchers toward other topics of inquiry. Clearly, strong levels of insight into lived experiences of individuals can be gained by using first-person perspectives.

Hurlbutt and Chalmers (2002) interviewed three adults with ASD. The researchers also examined the individuals' published and unpublished works to explore perceptions of their own life experiences. A common theme from all three individuals was frustration with perceived narrowmindedness of neurotypical (NT) people. The first participant stated, "most people with autism get frustrated with NTs because very often, it's the so-called 'normal' people who lack empathy because many of them don't want to listen to any point of view besides their own" (Hurlbutt & Chalmers, 2002, p. 106). The second participant said, "one of my friends divides NTs into two categories: High Functioning, such as yourself, and Low Functioning, who do not understand us. This is a joke, but it shows my belief in this subject" (Hurlbutt & Chalmers, 2002, p. 106). The third participant stated, "I am tired of having to do 100 % of the changing, and there is no change with most people without autism" (Hurlbutt & Chalmers, 2002, p. 106).

Traditional mechanisms of education research alone, by which researchers observe autistic people and are often looking for specific stereotypical behaviors related to autism, would have fallen short in accessing these insightful thoughts and attitudes toward neurotypicals. There was a sense of frustration felt through these quotes, and this is what researchers and clinicians must work to address. By using first-person perspective from Adam's story, and examining previously written autobiographies, I transcended traditional modes of education research.

Autobiographical Research

Though well intentioned, researchers have often perpetuated stereotypes of autism without realizing it. For example, in 1986, Dr. Temple Grandin published her book, *Emergence: Labeled Autistic*. This autobiography, written by an autistic individual, was the first of its kind. The foreword of the book was written by Dr. Bernard Rimland, a research psychologist who had a son with ASD. In the foreword, Rimland expressed doubt Grandin had autism based on her ability to communicate clearly with him, which reflects the stereotype people with autism are not as competent as their neurotypical peers. When addressing her interest in psychology, he wrote, "Those who do [go to college] usually major in math or computers, not psychology. And here she was, telephoning and planning to visit another city on her own. Such competence is extremely rare in autistic persons" (Grandin & Scariano, 1986, p. 2). The idea people with autism only excel in fields related to math and technology has remained a prevalent stereotype. Rimland went on to write:

> Here was an individual who recognized that she had oddities and peculiarities of speech and manner as a result of her affliction with autism, but who took them as a matter of course, and regarded them as obstacles to be overcome, rather than reasons to be self- conscious or embarrassed. (Grandin & Scariano, 1986, p. 2)

Although this statement was intended as a compliment, it reflected a condescending attitude toward autism, which has long been considered an affliction and an obstacle rather than a difference in demeanor and understanding of the world. His statement also implied Grandin's behaviors were something most others would be "embarrassed" by, perpetuating social hierarchy between people with ASD and those without. Toward the end of the foreword, Rimland recounted speaking to Grandin several years after their first encounter, "impressed with how much less autistic-sounding" she was (Grandin & Scariano, 1986, p. 3). This statement again supported the attitude autism is something to be overcome, rather than understood and accepted. Though Rimland spoke highly of Grandin and her accomplishments, he mostly spoke of her in terms of her autism, and his writing reflected problematic stereotypes.

In contrast to the foreword, Grandin's account of her experiences captured readers' attention in a way traditional academic writing cannot. She took readers inside her head, allowing us the privilege of being privy to her innermost thoughts and understanding her experiences in a remarkable way. For example, she described a childhood incident when her mom drove her to speech therapy and they got into a car accident. She typically did not speak much at this young age, but as window glass shattered, she was able to clearly say "ice ice ice" in reference to the shards of glass (Grandin & Scariano, 1986, p. 14). She described being able to speak during the accident because situational stress overcame barriers usually inhibiting her from speaking. In another childhood experience, she was unable to clap along to the beat of a piano while her class learned about rhythm. Ultimately, Grandin's teacher directed her to leave her hands in her lap because she was "spoiling it for everyone" (Grandin & Scariano, 1986, p. 26).

Other students laughed at her inability to clap with them, and Grandin jumped off her chair in frustration and anger, knocking the chair over in the process. Subsequently, the teacher made Grandin stand in the corner until the rhythm exercise was complete. As Grandin explained, engaging in two motor tasks at the same time was simply challenging for her, which contributed to clapping out of sync during that exercise.

A classroom observer would not have been able to gain this insight without Grandin's storytelling. Her ability and willingness to share her story as an adult allowed readers to understand how her childhood experiences shaped her identity and worldview as an adult. For many children, regardless of an autism diagnosis, it is difficult to understand and evaluate experiences as they occur. As an adult, reflecting back on these experiences allows the author to describe them in a thorough way. Grandin went on to describe her life experiences as an "abyss of aloneness" (Grandin & Scariano, 1986, p. 15). Like Adam, Grandin stated she chose to share her story to offer hope to parents and professionals, thereby countering sustained stereotypes associated with autistic adults.

Study Objectives

The research objectives of this study were to (a) understand experiences and needs of autistic people as they transition to adulthood; (b) gain this understanding by directly speaking to someone on the spectrum and examining autobiographies, memoirs, life histories, and literature produced by autistic adults; and (c) disseminate information that challenges and ultimately expands upon existing literature on how to best support autistic adults as they navigate complexities of adulthood. In Adam's own words, we conducted this research together, because:

> I get told that I'm an inspiration and I bring hope to mental health consumers and parents and autism parents. When I used to attend A Heart to Heart with Mom Meetup group, those were Autism parents, they said I gave them a lot of hope. So, what I hope to achieve by writing this book is to spread that same hope to a broader range of people, who I may never meet face to face. When I tell them what I'm doing with my life, they admit that they didn't think someone with this condition could do most of this because of the media stereotypes and portrayals. I want to break the stereotypes.
>
> I am writing this book with Sneha, who to me represents an autism advocate.
>
> Sneha approached me to write this book to help understand the needs of autistic folks like me as we transition to adulthood. I didn't really want to discuss my diagnosis until adulthood, when I started living my all-play, no-work lifestyle that I believe most people in Orange County, California despised me for. Now I want to educate people on how difficult it actually is for someone with autism to make money and be accepted in the neurotypical mainstream workplace and society. I use the term "neurotypical" to refer

to people who are not diagnosed with Autism Spectrum Disorders. Sneha helped me put my story into words, and I am proud of my story and my life. (A. P. Valerius, personal communication, April 9, 2018)

In contrast to the majority of existing literature, this research used the social model of disability and first-person perspectives to offer a different understanding of needs, supports, and services for autistic adults as they transition to adulthood. By learning directly from autistic adults, this study illustrated the role society plays in perpetuating notions of disability and offered insights on how we can better adapt to different needs, rather than putting the burden of change on autistic people. As demonstrated by Adam's excerpt in the introduction, his story articulated experiences not previously spoken about to foster deeper understanding. By structuring our research in this way, Adam and I hoped to inform service providers, academics, employers, parents, and society at large about lived experiences of autistic people, allowing for greater inclusion and participation in the community during adulthood. Furthermore, Adam's story was coconstructed by Adam and myself; I spent several years gaining Adam's trust and learning his story.

To add to dominant modes of educational research, rather than solely conducting a literature review of articles in peer-reviewed journals, I also gathered data in the form of published autobiographies, memoirs, and first-person stories written by autistic people. I conducted a content analysis of these books to glean emergent themes from individuals' stories.

By including voices of autistic individuals, I honored my commitment to represent these individuals as experts in their own lives, navigating their experiences, hopes, fears, and desires to create future supports *with* them rather than *for* them. Though each individual has their own unique experiences, which prohibited generalization to everyone with an autism diagnosis, I was able to integrate Adam's story in a relatable, accessible way by analyzing emergent themes from several additional stories.

This book was developed in three parts. Part One includes Chapter One, the introduction, and Chapter Two, the methodology and theoretical framework. Part Two is Adam's story, relayed in chronological order from childhood to his most recent adulthood experiences. Part Three includes the findings of this study. The themes are defined and experiential examples for each theme are reflected by Adam's stories and the studied autobiographies. Presenting Adam's story as its own major section provides an immersive look into Adam's life as expressed in his own words. The thematic analysis in Part Three contains critical examples from the autobiographies to support each theme Adam's story presented. Additionally, as I analyzed and identified various themes, I also conducted targeted literature reviews for each theme; I integrated this literature with first-person experiences from the autobiographies. This allowed me to recognize similarities and differences among autistic individuals' experiences, and similarities and differences between traditional empirical research and first-person narrative. Part Three of this book combined more traditional research foundations from Part One and nontraditional information presented in Part Two to discuss my findings and future application of them to create a more inclusive society.

I located 53 books that fit my general search criteria: autobiographical accounts of adults with ASD. Of the 53 books, 20 were chosen for analysis. Inclusion criteria for books included those written or narrated by an autistic adult or, if written by multiple family members, the focus had to address lived experiences of the autistic individual. Additionally, the book had to be autobiographical in nature (rather than books containing advice). Finally, if multiple autobiographical books were written by the same author, I chose the most recently published book for review.

The 33 books excluded from this study were formatted as advice or "how to" books rather than autobiographical accounts of lived experiences, or were written by academics, therapists, or family members. A few were also written together with family members but lacked the central narrative of an autistic person's voice. Similarly, a number of books were formatted as a collection of stories by multiple people, rather than one person's narrative. Lastly, if the same author wrote multiple books, I chose the most recent book with autobiographical content, thereby naturally excluding previous works.

Although 33 books did not satisfy inclusion criteria for my study, they were and should still be considered important resources for insights into lived experiences of autistic people.

Because there have been so few books written using first-person perspectives of autistic people, three of the 20 books included were written by individuals under the age of 18. Adam's story also included childhood memories and experiences, so perspectives from children on the spectrum added to insights from Adam's childhood. Table 4 contains a detailed table with information about the 20 books chosen for this study.

Conclusion

This study impacts people in academic and nonacademic settings. As described in the literature review, limited search results reflected a significant void in research pertaining to ASD, adult transitional needs, and ASD-related human experiences, such as hopes, dreams, aspirations, and everyday challenges. With this research, therapists and other health professionals will be provided information directly from the source; these insights are essential and, yet, still underdeveloped. Professionals could then disseminate this information to their communities, which could allow for greater acceptance and awareness of autistic adult needs. Professionals could also use this information to better tailor services to autistic adults.

Voices of autistic people have continued to be minimized as researchers and medical practitioners create services *for* them rather than collaborate *with* them. With the publication of her book, Grandin was one of the first recognized autistic people to engage in self-advocacy and counter many stereotypes associated with ASD (Grandin & Scariano, 1986). The publication of her book represented a turning point for understanding ASD. The next autobiography by an autistic person was not published until Williams (1992), and though there are now more published autobiographies and memoirs, they remain scarce and often neglected in academic research.

This research study targeted a number of problems, including lack of adequate literature describing needs for autistic adults, lack of literature using first-person perspectives of autistic people, and the tendency of existing literature to perpetuate stereotypes of ASD rather than humanize autistic individuals. My research challenged dominant modes of education research by seeking to understand lived experiences of autistic people, and I gained these insights by speaking directly with an autistic individual, examining literature directly produced by autistic adults, and disseminating this information in book format, which can increase accessibility to diverse groups of readers.

Chapter Two

Methodology and Theoretical Framework

Although qualitative research (narrative inquiry included) is now more accepted in research circles, it was not originally viewed as legitimate education research. Anderson and Herr (1999), however, noted the value of narrative inquiry in the field:

> The problems faced by professional schools such as colleges of education are complex, since members of these communities must legitimize themselves to an environment which includes both a university culture that values basic research and theoretical knowledge and a professional culture of schooling that values applied research and narrative knowledge. (p. 12)

In relation to autism research, "basic research" refers to quantitative research, statistical studies, and applied behavior analysis, in that these "basic research" philosophies focus on the importance of objectivity. The notion of objectivity—combined with clear parameters of what defines validity in quantitative research—has always been appealing, and thus set university research standards for years. According to Schön (1995), adopting technical rationality was necessary for admittance into professional schools and research universities.

Whereas qualitative researchers have historically had to conform to quantitative standards, there is now abundant research that supports, and even encourages, use of qualitative practices in education research.

According to Ferguson and Ferguson (2000), "by addressing dimensions of quality rather than a universal standard of acceptability, a pluralistic approach to inquiry can nourish both creativity and utility" (p. 180) when it comes to qualitative research. As Anderson and Herr (1999) noted, one of the biggest shortcomings of quantitative research is it fails to include research participants' voices and perspectives. This exclusion is problematic; by not including those with the highest stakes in the research, doubts arise over the actual goal of the research.

Does the research actually benefit participants, or does the research simply function to bolster the researcher's status? Quantitative research can also be problematic because it assumes complete objectivity actually exists. The reality of researcher bias challenges that assumption (Anderson & Herr, 1999). As acceptance of qualitative research increases, researchers must redefine and reconceptualize what entails rigorous knowledge and recognize qualitative methodology as a different type of methodology with its own standards to adhere to, rather than trying to make qualitative methodology adhere to quantitative expectations.

This chapter explores how I, as researcher, collaborated with Adam, my coresearcher, using narrative methodology and a social model of disability framework to conduct our research through Adam's story. Our research objectives involved the following: (a) gain understanding of autistic individuals' experiences and needs as they transition into adulthood; (b) develop this understanding using the first-person perspective of someone on the spectrum and examining autobiographies, memoirs, life histories, and literature produced by autistic adults; and (c) disseminate results that challenge and expand upon prior literature on how best to support adults with ASD.

If we allow personal stories of people with disabilities to inform society through life histories, memoirs, narratives, and other mechanisms, these stories could potentially act as "intervention into the politics of knowing and the politics of representation" (Ferri, 2011, p. 2279). As Tillman (2002) explained, conducting socially sensitive research can catalyze educational change. This is ultimately what Adam and I hoped to achieve; through collaboration, we used Adam's insider perspective to enlighten society about actual trials and triumphs of autistic people.

Trustworthiness

Developing a high-quality qualitative study required consideration of its trustworthiness. One factor of a trustworthy study, as explained by Ferguson and Ferguson (2000), is importance of context and relations in qualitative research. The authors noted, "in a methodology where knowledge and meaning are constructed through social interaction and understanding, the relationships that occur between researchers and participants are critical" (Ferguson & Ferguson, 2000, p. 183). To summarize, researchers must ensure they adequately developed a relationship strong enough to collect trustworthy information from research participants. Ferguson and Ferguson even asserted many good studies start by asking one question, only to realize there are more relevant questions to ask. They made this discovery in a process of meaningful coconstruction with their research participants.

Another dimension of trustworthiness in qualitative research is utility and relevance.

Ferguson and Ferguson (2000) described four types of utility: (a) instrumental utility: does the research allow knowledge gained to apply to a specific problem?; (b) enlightenment utility: how does the research benefit us? For example, do we gain greater understanding of a phenomenon, or greater insight of the studied problem?; (c) symbolic utility: how does the research make sense of information previously not known to us?; and (d) emancipatory utility: "research can be useful in challenging the structures, policies, and practices that disempower and marginalize entire segments of the population" (p. 184).

Two other components of trustworthiness strengthening qualitative research are reciprocity (Harrison et al., 2001) and fidelity (Moss, 2004). Harrison (2001) provided a strong description of reciprocity:

> Reciprocity, the give and take of social interactions, may be used to gain access to a particular setting. Through judicious use of self-disclosure, interviews become conversations, and richer data are possible. By asking participants to

examine field notes and early analyses, researchers can give back something to their participants and engage in member checks as a means of ensuring trustworthiness. (p. 323)

Reciprocity is important when examining issues and dynamics of power in the researcher–participant relationship. A thorough appreciation for and understanding of the researcher–participant relationship is critical in qualitative research. Blumenfeld-Jones (1995, as cited in Moss, 2004), stated, "Fidelity, another measure of trustworthiness in narrative research . . . evaluates the quality of the resultant narratives and provided me with a tool for social action for altering inequitable social relations" (p. 364). In other words, one role of trustworthiness is providing evidence of research accountability and shared responsibility.

In my research with Adam, I used several components of qualitative research to ensure trustworthiness. I took (and still take) responsibility of sharing Adam's life story seriously.

Adam and I collaborated to coconstruct his story, and Adam read the final research project in its entirety to ensure his story remained authentic when integrated with other autobiographies.

Gaining Adam's feedback was a form of member checking, which ensured my interpretation of data captured Adam's message and voice in the final presentation (Creswell & Poth, 2018).

Member checking helps strengthen believability of research and is a crucial step in qualitative research (Creswell & Poth, 2018).

Remaining central to trustworthy research, I also included (and amplified) Adam's voice. By using what Harrison et al. (2001) termed "reciprocity," I constantly checked in with Adam to provide updates on our research. I typed his story as he spoke to me, and then I gave it to him to read and make sure everything was written as he intended. With his permission, I edited portions of his writing; for example, I moved parts of his story around to allow narrative to flow more sensibly and requested Adam check and approve of every edit I made. Again, my goal was to ensure his story continued to represent his voice.

As Moss's (2004) tenet of fidelity described, I ensured Adam's story was told in a meaningful way while treating him with respect throughout the process. I defined "meaningful way" as the way in which he controlled the process; he was able to share his story with the world in a way he felt comfortable. For example, toward the end of our meetings, he preferred I refrained from typing while he spoke. Instead, we set my laptop next to us and turned on the "dictation" option in Microsoft Word, which typed as Adam spoke. Doing so allowed me to focus more on our conversations, but also required combing through transcripts following our conversations to edit parts inaccurately dictated. Adam also preferred to discuss some topics via email instead of verbally, which allowed him to experience a different level of catharsis while writing about his experiences.

Adam had the largest stake in the outcome of this research, as he invested his time and shared deeply personal stories. As such, he was included as an equal partner in the research process. While developing the narrative, he preferred I ask him questions to which he could respond. Adam found it difficult to retrieve memories on his own, so asking him questions helped refresh his memory. Although I came equipped with general questions to start our conversations, I also tried to ask open-ended and follow-up questions based on topics Adam brought up. Adam was an equal partner in terms of deciding what was included, what specifics were discussed, and how the research would be distributed. I acknowledge Adam's story became a coconstruction of knowledge, as we collaborated to share his story. The experiences he shared were shaped by questions I asked and how I presented his story.

I also remained cognizant my personal knowledge of autism and adulthood, which I initially gained from an educational background in psychology and applied behavior analysis, changed dramatically following Adam's firsthand accounts about transitioning to adulthood while on the autism spectrum. For example, my training in applied behavior analysis focused on early intervention as a means to help autistic individuals learn socially acceptable behaviors, thus being able to more successfully serve their communities. After my conversations with Adam, however, I learned autistic adults have different needs and supports from what we have targeted with early intervention, which has largely addressed child and adolescent needs and could not guarantee higher success or adaptability as autistic adults. More specifically, this knowledge demonstrated what Ferguson and Ferguson (2002) described as instrumental utility and emancipatory utility: this research can allow us to change well-meaning but sometimes demeaning support services offered to adults with autism.

Bishop (2005) created guidelines to ensure researchers monitor their own sense of power and control when conducting responsible research. The components included examining how research was initiated; who will benefit from the research; whose ideas and experiences are represented; whose needs, interests, and concerns the research represents (legitimation); and who holds researchers accountable. Reality is a constantly evolving phenomenon and must be discovered and interpreted together. By truly getting to know research participants' stories, researchers are able to share their truths.

Following Bishop's (2005) guidelines, I further enhanced trustworthiness of my research by ensuring sense of power and control were in check. First, this study was initiated after many adults with ASD reached out to me, expressing frustrations about their inability to obtain or keep a long-term job, prompting me to approach Adam and ask more about his experiences. His enthusiasm led to our mutual decision to write a book together; we wanted to help others who may relate to him and professionals who may benefit from his direct insights. Ideas and experiences represented in this book are directly those of Adam's, an autistic adult. Additionally, I included experiences of other adults who have written or documented first-person accounts. I endeavored to represent needs, interests, concerns, fears, desires, and hopes of adults on the autism spectrum, but always kept their wellbeing in mind. Finally, I was held accountable by Adam as I helped him tell his story on his terms. Moreover, I can be held accountable by every single person who has received an ASD diagnosis or relates to this diagnosis. I recognize readers may generalize themes to anyone they know with autism, so I take responsibility to represent Adam's truth seriously.

Research Questions

The central research question guiding my research was: What are the lived experiences of autistic adults? As I cultivated my research, I developed more specific research questions:

1. What did Adam's story tell us about:
   a. The lives of autistic people?
   b. Societal and structural responses to autism?
2. How do experiences described in autobiographical literature by autistic adults support, refute, exemplify, or amplify Adam's experiences?

Theoretical Framework: Social Model of Disability

Historically, disability has been defined by the medical model, which emphasizes a deficit-based perspective on disability. This study, however, was guided by the social model of disability, which is supported by the field of disability studies (DS). DS reconceptualizes disability as meaningful in social, political, and cultural contexts without denying physiological aspects of impaired functions (Baglieri et al., 2011; Siebers, 2011). The social model of disability challenges the medical model of disability that has shaped people's experiences for so long. DS is rooted in activism of people with disabilities and has influenced social and political views on disability (Baglieri et al., 2011; Siebers, 2011). The major tenets of the social model of disability are:

- Disability is a minority identity and a product of social injustice. Disability is not a product of individual defect. Instead, it can be reclaimed as a positive identity and contribution to society. This is not to say disabled individuals overlook benefits of specific or different supports; rather, the notion of "disability" simply serves to pathologize some of these differences.
- Disability is a social construct defining certain functions as normal and others as disability. Baglieri et al. (2011) noted, "to call

or think of some of those differences as 'disabilities' is to make a social judgment, not a neutral or value-free observation" (p. 270).
- Though only certain functions are termed "disability," many people need supports to enhance functioning across a wide spectrum of activities (e.g., physical, social, emotional, cognitive). Challenging construction of disability does not mean we ignore respective supports everyone needs to participate in society. In other words, impairments exist, but there are differences between providing supports for impairments and viewing differences caused by impairments as a disability.
- Social construction of disability reflects the dominant "able" person's societal structure and influence; this able mindedness creates advantages for certain physical, social, emotional, and cognitive abilities. For example, an able-bodied person may design a building with good intentions—including creating necessary accommodations for a wheelchair user in the building's bathroom—but does not include a curb cut for the wheelchair user on the sidewalk leading to the building's bathroom. Another example stems from medical professionals using DSM-5 criteria to treat autistic people. The DSM-5 was written by neurotypical people who have not lived with autism, thus autism was presented as a set of deficits, rather than differences processing and relating to information.
- We should strive to include voices of people with disabilities in research as equal cocreators of knowledge. Nothing about us without us (Charlton, 1998), means voices of those with disabilities should be central in discussions of disability-related experiences and needs.
- Disability should be a civil rights issue in addition to a healthcare issue; the latter is how disability is perceived by society and, in many ways, by laws.

Disability has come to represent inability to engage in what society considers normal activities due to perceived deficits (Thomas, 2002). For example, ASD is listed in DSM-5 standards as a neurodevelopmental condition characterized by persistent deficits in social interactions, communication, and maintaining relationships. The medical model has been used to create diagnostic labels, which have influenced attitudes and interactions toward people labeled with ASD (Angulo-Jimenez & DeThorne, 2019). DS counters diagnostic labels, asserting disability is created when the nondisabled majority create barriers (both attitudinal and physical); these barriers limit the social activities in which a disabled person can engage. In this light, the term disability should be understood as a form of social oppression, similar to sexism and racism, rather than a sole medical concern (Charlton, 1998; Thomas, 2002). This research uses the social model of disability to reframe disability as a structural component of society with the understanding all people depend on each other to survive and thrive (Siebers, 2011).

DS strives to include voices of people with disabilities in disability-related research, which leads to equality, inclusion, and dignity. The field recognizes knowledge is based on perspective (Siebers, 2011). DS also acknowledges researchers construct knowledge about topics they study, as it can never be a completely objective process, and people with disabilities should be included in the construction of disability (Baglieri et al., 2011). After all, major stakeholders in this study—those with disabilities—should have their voices heard and shared. By definition, DS is not created solely by academic professionals, but rather by and alongside individuals forced to navigate ableist barriers and oppressions daily. DS intertwines individual experiences and activism with adjacent political and social influences (Thomas, 2002). This study uses the social model of disability to better explain social constructs of disability in relation to ASD by using insights directly from autistic adults and considering how to implement these concepts into everyday practices for teachers, therapists, researchers, and society. By centralizing voices of autistic authors, this book recognizes autistic adults are experts in their autism and collaboration with autistic adults is central to success of autism support and inclusion.

Furthermore, disability reflects a relationship between people with certain impairments and those without impairments; this relationship is evident in every aspect of life, including housing options, employment, healthcare, political rights, and education (Thomas, 2002). Siebers (2011) noted DS does not focus on treatment or cures but, rather, studies:

The social meanings, symbols, and stigmas attached to disability identity and asks how they relate to enforced systems of exclusion and oppression, attacking the widespread belief that an able body and mind determines whether one is a quality human being. (p. 3)

Rehabilitation often focuses on activities and treatment, allowing the disabled person to live as normal as possible because individual impairments have directly caused social disadvantages. DS encourages medical practitioners to instead view each person as a lived entity, not merely body parts with possible impairments (Thomas, 2002). This research study exemplifies how a person without certain impairments can cocreate research with a person who does have specific impairments. While this concept is discussed in detail in the researcher positionality section, it is important to note that Adam is an autistic adult and I am not, and this difference in backgrounds and life experiences has shaped our understanding of the world. In line with the social model of disability, this research respects each of our knowledge and experiences, and presents it as a combination of academic analysis and lived experience.

As Baglieri et al. (2011) explained, disability discrimination has not historically been considered a civil rights issue, despite causing oppression, segregation, dehumanization, and exploitation. Discrimination against disability is not easily recognized because disability is currently understood as a health and safety issue rather than an extension of one's identity. People should be judged on actions and opinions, but due to the ideology of ability, "individuals show themselves to be worthy of membership in civil society through the exercise of certain abilities. Human-rights discourse will never break free from the ideology of ability until it includes disability as a defining characteristic of human beings" (Siebers, 2011, p. 178). There is evidential inequity for disabled people as a minority identity, and there is no justification for differential treatment (Baglieri et al., 2011; Siebers, 2011).

DS stresses research should provide a platform for participants in a study. To enhance platform building via educational research, it should be a collaborative process in which, together, the researcher and participant steer the study to share how the participant experiences the world

(Berryman et al., 2013). Typically, participants are not included in the research process. Rather than a collaborative effort between researcher and participant, the participant is "studied" and has no further role. DS can be applied to any disability group. Individuals in these groups are often oppressed and suppressed in research because researchers exclude them from decision making. To help reverse this trend, I used the social model of disability to examine how autistic adults make sense of the world and define meaning in adulthood. I spent over 2 years conversing with Adam to learn directly from him, and I analyzed autobiographies of 20 autistic authors to ensure my own understanding of autistic life experiences was as thorough as possible. This study created a platform for autistic voices and will be disseminated in the form of a book to maximize access to this information.

Methodological Frameworks

As mentioned previously, this book uses first-person literature to understand lived experiences of adults with ASD. This use of qualitative research intentionally reflects how the social model of disability can be applied to research. More specifically, the qualitative methodology I used in this research were narrative inquiry and disability life writing.

Narrative Inquiry

The primary methodology used in my study was categorized as narrative inquiry.

Narrative inquiry is an interdisciplinary methodology influenced by literature, history, anthropology, sociology, psychology, and education (Creswell & Poth, 2018). To frame my research, I used Clandinin et al.'s (2017) definition of narrative inquiry:

> People shape their daily lives by stories of who they and others are and as they interpret their past in terms of these stories. Story, in the current idiom, is a portal through which a person enters the world and by which their

experience of the world is interpreted and made personally meaningful. (p. 90)

Rather than trying to fit neatly into a theory, narrative inquiry puts emphasis on the role of lived experiences, including all of a person's emotions, values, and experiences (Clandinin & Connelly, 2000). There is no fixed framework for narrative inquiry; rather, focus is on a person's experience and how their experiences are told:

> The contribution of a narrative inquiry is more often intended to be the creation of a new sense of meaning and significance with respect to the research topic than it is to yield a set of knowledge claims that might incrementally add to knowledge in the field. (Clandinin & Connelly, 2000, p. 42)

Narrative inquiry is best used when the researcher's aim is to capture in-depth stories from one individual or a small group of people and the researcher is able to dedicate an extended amount of time to spend with these individuals, which allows for data to be collected in multiple ways. For example, Adam and I met several times throughout the year to have our conversations, during which I transcribed his stories. In addition to these conversations, I also spent time engaging in activities considered important to him, including attending a National Alliance of Mental Illness (NAMI) support group at the wellness center he regularly attended. During this visit, I simply observed the support group alongside Adam. This allowed me to gain a different perspective and insight into topics I had not thought to ask him about before. During this group meeting, I shared I have Generalized Anxiety Disorder and have been going to therapy regularly for years. I believe my disclosure and shared experience in the support group allowed Adam to see me from a different perspective, as I humanized my own experiences and created a different bond between us, rather than maintaining our relationship as one solely of researcher and coresearcher.

Narrative inquiry is also best used when the researcher includes contextual information about the participant's stories, including the individual's culture, time period in their life, and settings in which their experiences took place. Clandinin and Connelly (2000) referred to this as "three-dimensional narrative inquiry space" (p. 49), in which the researcher intertwines personal and social elements (interaction); past, present, and future circumstances (continuity); and information on place (situation) in the participant's story. In addition, the researcher must acknowledge collaboration in narrative inquiry. Without the research participant, narrative inquiry is simply not possible, which reiterates the need for researcher and participant to be equal coconstructors of generated knowledge. While engaging in narrative inquiry, the relationship between researcher and participant is paramount, and both individuals change, learn, and grow throughout the process. Finally, the purpose of using narrative inquiry is to amplify voices of individuals who otherwise may not be heard. Thus, once a person's stories and experiences are collected, they must be integrated into a meaningful story, highlighting their experiences and the larger social, cultural, and political contexts in which these experiences took place (Clandinin et al., 2017; Clandinin & Connelly, 2000; Creswell & Poth, 2018; Riessman, 2008).

With narrative inquiry, the researcher collects stories directly from individuals on their lived experiences and examines these experiences through social, cultural, familial, and institutional contexts of the time period (Creswell & Poth, 2018). Stories collected through narrative inquiry often shed light on how the participant views themself or views various societal issues. Timing also provides important contextual information for individual experiences (Creswell & Poth, 2018). Once the researcher collects data—which can be gathered in the form of structured interviews, casual conversations, attended events, or photographs—data can be shaped into a chronological story to help make sense of the individual's experiences (Clandinin & Connelly, 2000; Creswell & Poth, 2018).

Narrative research builds a story from coconstruction of knowledge between the researcher and participant. Although the participant shares their stories, narrative often develops in response to questions or comments from the researcher, which influences what or how a story is told (Creswell & Poth, 2018; Riessman, 2008). Additionally, although stories are the participant's, it is usually the researcher who chronologically restructures these individual stories into a more holistic story of the participant's life—even if not exactly how the stories were originally delivered. The shaping of a chronological story is considered a form of structural analysis. Another common form of analysis in narrative inquiry is thematic analysis, which involves the researcher looking for common themes throughout the participant's individual stories and interviews (Creswell & Poth, 2018; Riessman, 2008). Finally, dialogic analysis focuses on how the story is produced and shared. For example, exchanges can emerge through formal interviews or casual conversations, and stories can then be published in academic journals, books, or performed as plays. Analysis type depends on the nature of participant experiences, the form of data collection, and the intended audience for the end product (Creswell & Poth, 2018; Riessman, 2008).

Narrative inquiry can also tell more than one person's story. Narrative inquiry takes the individual's story and presents it in ways used to strengthen group identities and encourage political and societal change, especially for those belonging to marginalized groups (Creswell & Poth, 2018). The emphasis on human rights in narrative inquiry allows this methodology to influence social justice research in a nontraditional way, with participant voices and experiences centered (Caine et al., 2018). Whereas social justice research usually begins by examining specifically problematic policies, narrative inquiry examines individual's stories, and themes emerging from these stories may inherently uncover problematic societal practices and attitudes. By understanding our research participants' perspectives and experiences, we gain insight into problems not yet specifically labeled. In this light, engaging in narrative inquiry is a form of social justice practice (Caine et al., 2018). The study of human experience is one of the worthiest topics to understand (Ashby & Causton-Theoharis, 2009), and this is exactly what narrative inquiry allows us to do. With our work, Adam and I hope to inspire social change. As articulated in Adam's own words:

> I get told that I'm an inspiration and I bring hope to mental health consumers, parents, and autism parents. What I hope to achieve by writing this book is to spread that same hope to a broader range of people, who I may never meet face to face. When I tell some people what I'm doing with my life they admit that they didn't think someone with this condition could do most of this because of the media stereotypes and portrayals of autism. I want to

break the stereotypes. I want to educate people on how difficult it actually is for someone with autism to make money and be accepted in the neurotypical mainstream workplace and society. (A. P. Valerius, personal communication, November 17, 2018)

Disability Life Writing

According to findings from Couser (2004), the form of research Adam and I conducted could be further categorized as disability life writing, which refers to a form of writing in which disabled people share their personal experiences. This sharing is done to challenge predominant and oppressive definitions of disability and shine a light on the social and political nature of disabilities. By including fiction, film, popular culture, and first-person narratives into DS education, conversations about disabilities as a deficit morph into more of an accepting model based on relational discourse (Ferri, 2011). Ferri (2011) stated, "disability life writing locates disability as a complex social, political, and embodied position from which an individual might legitimately narrate his/her life experience" (p. 2268). What Ferri meant by this is disability life writing allows society to view disability and ability as socially constructed concepts of normalcy, preventing people from oppressing those labeled with a disability.

Disability is not only a personal experience, but a social one as well. Autobiographical works or narratives by disabled people have potential to challenge societal meanings dictated to disability and highlight social and political roles defining disability with facts based on personal experiences (Ferri, 2011). This phenomenon is illustrated in Part Two, as many of the autobiographical authors reflected on how they modified their behavior depending on societal expectations throughout different time periods. By collaborating with Adam and presenting his story together, Adam and I hope to change society's perception and understanding of ASD. We hope this book relates to autistic individuals and motivates them to continue pursuing their strengths and passions, rather than focusing on what society has labeled deficits. We hope to change society's understanding of ASD and defy the perception autistic people must change who they are to fit in.

Because Adam and I worked together to tell his story, we used the social model of disability lens to coconstruct a new narrative helping to make sense of life on the spectrum. Furthermore, rather than simply explaining the social model of disability, we actually used it in our research by providing a platform for voices of many autistic authors. There has been a growing body of autism-related autobiographical literature, and this research adds to this literature while analyzing it in relation to others.

Data Collection

I conducted approximately 40 semistructured interviews with the goal of encapsulating important aspects of the transition to adulthood amid life on the spectrum. I phrase this number as "approximately" 40 because some correspondence was conducted via back-and-forth emails, as per Adam's request. "Interviews" were more akin to conversations between two colleagues. By the time we began this research project, Adam and I had worked together for over a year, and we knew each other well. We supported each other in our professional endeavors and had already developed mutual respect and friendship. When we first met and began working together, our relationship was more professional, but over time our professional relationship evolved into a friendship. Our conversations felt natural, as we met at Starbucks or sandwich places for lunch and chatted or went to events that we both were interested in, to expand our social networking skills. I kept an open mind during my conversations with Adam to catch developing themes. I met with Adam approximately once a week for about 2 hours, and those meetings spanned 1 year. Occasionally, Adam and I would communicate via phone or email.

Meetings continued until I collected adequate information, but Adam and I remain friends and catch up over coffee or skype. During the coronavirus pandemic, we often checked in on each other and during the toilet paper shortage that took over the nation I went to Adam's home and dropped off some extra toilet paper for him. After that incident, Adam's Mom kindly texted me to thank me for looking out for her son. Adam has met my husband and my son as well, and our friendship and mutual respect for each other has allowed us to create and present our knowledge together.

Whereas scholarly literature on adulthood has focused largely on life events, such as employment, living situations, college experiences, and relationships, in our cocreated research we used Adam's definition of adulthood:

> To me, adulthood is freedom and independence, like you're finally in control of your own life instead of someone else controlling your life for you. Responsibilities come with the freedom and independence, but adulthood is being able to handle those responsibilities.
>
> Independence is like getting to see the doctor without your parents right there. Having a bank account that they don't have access to. Paying your own rent and bills. (A. P. Valerius, personal communication, November 17, 2018)

Though Adam knew he had the option to end the research at any time, he chose to continue. Sometimes, I could tell Adam was upset while discussing painful memories, and on those occasions, I would end the research portion of our conversation early and transition to more neutral topics.

Additional information was gathered in the form of autobiographical literature directly produced by people with ASD. After analyzing the autobiographical research, I discovered common themes and trends of adulthood as defined directly by people on the spectrum. By collecting and including additional information about autistic people's experiences, I ensured our book's relatability. I had intentionally accomplished what Ferguson and Ferguson (2000) referred to as contextualizing; I connected one story to many current stories of people with ASD to explore common cultural identity and experiences.

This contextualization was important because voices of people on the spectrum are often not used in research. Instead, parents or siblings may write about their familial experiences. By gathering and disseminating information directly from those on the spectrum, scholar-practitioners in this field can better understand life experiences and needs for those with autism. Furthermore, this research will be distributed in the form of a book anyone can buy, not a peer- reviewed academic journal, which often requires high subscription fees and is inaccessible to most people outside academia. By disseminating the research in book form, other autistic adults will be able to access and perhaps relate to it; family members of autistic individuals will be able to read the book and perhaps view their child's experiences from a different vantage point; employers, teachers, and therapists may gain further insights for their research or teaching; and any person who picks up the book can learn more about life with ASD.

Data Analysis

After several in-person and phone conversations with Adam throughout 2018 and 2019, data began to get saturated, an indication we were ready for the next step in our research: data analysis. My interview transcriptions with Adam were 54 pages long, single spaced. Rearranging my conversations with Adam into story form could be considered a type of descriptive coding, which was helpful to organize Adam's experiences and stories as a whole; however, descriptive coding does not offer any analytic insight (Saldaña, 2016).

Through analytic coding, researchers are able to look for patterns and figure out why they exist. Essentially, codes are links between data collection and explanation of meaning. The focus of my analysis was Adam's story, for which I used the grounded analysis portion of grounded theory. I then used the constant comparison method to analyze autobiographies written by other individuals on the spectrum to "deliberately search for commonalities throughout the data and use an evolving repertoire of established code" (Saldaña, 2016, p. 79). In doing so, I discovered patterns and insights representing the autism community as a whole, rather than solely Adam's experiences.

Grounded Theory Analysis

Grounded theory analysis is inductive, comparative, emergent, open ended, and flexible (Charmaz, 2012). Coding leads to "generalizable theoretical statements that transcend specific times and places and contextual analysis of actions and events" (Charmaz, 2012, p. 113). Coding is a "researcher generated construct that translates the data and attributes interpreted meaning and leads to pattern detection, categorization, and theory building" (Vogt et al., 2014, p. 13).

From codes we gain themes, which "bring meaning and identity to a recurrent (patterned) experience and captures/unifies the natures/basis of experience into a meaningful whole" (Saldaña, 2016, p. 199). These codes and themes then lead to theories, old or new, and allow for a more thorough understanding of setting, contexts, and participants, while helping predict and explain human actions (Saldaña, 2016).

Grounded theory analysis can be broken down into two coding cycles. First-cycle coding methods include attribute coding, in vivo coding, process coding, and initial (open) coding. First-cycle coding involves splitting data into individually coded segments. Second-cycle coding methods include focused coding, axial coding, and theoretical (selective) coding. Second-cycle coding methods include "constantly comparing, reorganizing, focusing the codes into categories, prioritizing them to develop 'axis' categories around which other categories revolve and synthesize them to formulate a central category that becomes the foundation for explication of a grounded theory" (Saldaña, 2016, p. 55). The first-cycle coding process helps reorganize data to develop a smaller and more select list of broader categories, themes, and concepts. The second-cycle coding process develops a sense of categorical, thematic, conceptual, and theoretical organization from first-cycle codes (Charmaz, 2012; Saldaña, 2016).

Attribute Coding

First-cycle coding begins with attribute coding, by which the researcher logs essential, descriptive information about data and participant demographic characteristics. This coding is effective for creating systems of data management and contexts for data analysis (Saldaña, 2016). I engaged in attribute coding at the very beginning of my conversations with Adam and included them in my researcher positionality statement, where I described my and Adam's backgrounds.

Initial (Open) Coding

Initial coding breaks qualitative data into parts and examines them for similarities and differences. Initial coding allows the researcher to remain open to all theoretical directions interpretation of data may evoke. Specifically, initial coding allows the researcher to "search for the properties and dimensions of categories-conceptual ideas that bring together similarly coded and related passages of data" (Saldaña, 2016, p. 118). Initial coding also enables the researcher to "study fragments of data (words, lines, segments, and incidents) closely for their analytic import" (Charmez, 2012, p. 109). As such, initial coding is a good starting point for analysis.

Once initial coding is complete, the researcher can engage in other first-cycle coding procedures, such as process coding or in vivo coding (Charmaz, 2012; Saldaña, 2016). I employed the initial coding technique when I read through transcripts of conversations with Adam and noticed there were common themes evident from our conversations. I restructured the conversations into story form to then engage in additional levels of coding.

In Vivo Coding

In vivo coding draws from participants' own language. One example includes using a word or short phrase from the participant's actual language when creating codes. In vivo coding is good to use when studying marginalized groups whose voices are often unheard, because using their actual words enhances and deepens understanding of their worldview. These codes help capture what is significant to the research participant and preserve meanings of their words and actions in actual code (Charmaz, 2012; Saldaña, 2016). When taking notes and coding, I tried to describe concepts in Adam's own words as much as possible. For example, I referred to those who have not been diagnosed with ASD as "neurotypicals." Additionally, during axial coding, I used Adam's own words to categorize his experiences as "isolation" and "empowerment." I also used NVivo software and conducted a word frequency query to capture the 100 most frequently used words in Adam's story.

Figure 1. NVivo Coding Word Cloud

This extra step ensured I would use Adam's own words in my codes. Figure 1 is a word map illustrating some of the most frequently used words in his story.

Process Coding

Process coding can happen at the same time as initial, focused, and axial coding and uses gerunds (-ing words) exclusively for codes. For example, observable activities would be expressed as "reading or playing," and conceptual concepts would be expressed as "adapting or struggling." The intent behind process coding is to look for consequences of action–interaction. Process coding is not a static description; rather, this type of coding provides a dynamic account of events based on movement or change over time, identifies what slows or accelerates the process, and determines under what conditions the process changes (Charmaz, 2012; Saldaña, 2016). During my initial coding, I made sure to use process coding by including gerunds for initial codes, such as "living," "seeking," "struggling," "understanding," "socializing," "feeling," and "taking."

Emotion Coding

Saldaña (2016) stated, "Emotions are a universal human experience and our acknowledgment of them in our research provides deep insight into the participants' perspectives, worldviews, and life conditions" (p. 125). Exploring Adam's inter/intrapersonal experiences and actions helped us understand how they influence his reactions, reasoning, decision making, judgment, and risk taking. Furthermore, a person's underlying emotions may reflect underlying attitudes of society (Saldaña, 2016). Though Adam's narrative did not always depict the emotional feelings he displayed, I noted when Adam seemed to respond strongly to certain topics during our conversations. This information helped me during coding because combining his words with emotions allowed me to better understand the impact certain experiences had on him. For example, a common misconception is people with ASD do not need or want social connections or relationships. Adam, however, often displayed strong emotions when he spoke about his relationship with his parents or desire for a romantic relationship. Adam was very insightful of his experiences, and he described emotions during those parts of his story, using words such as "hated," "full of tension," and "upsetting" when discussing his childhood relationship with his parents. He also mentioned he "got angrier than most people get when getting yelled at." He often described his attempted experience with friendships as making him feel "hopeless," "isolated," and, at times, "very depressed."

Focused (Selective) Coding

Focused (or selective) coding begins the second-cycle coding process by "using the most significant or frequent initial codes to sort, synthesize, integrate, and organize large amounts of data" (Charmaz, 2012, p. 113). Focused coding categorizes data based on thematic or conceptual similarity and forces the researcher to select which initial codes to include or expand upon (Charmaz, 2012; Saldaña, 2016). After my initial coding, I restructured conversations into story form, and categorized the following codes:

METHODOLOGY AND THEORETICAL FRAMEWORK

A. Diagnosis and treatments
   a. Hospitalizations and medications
      i. Struggling throughout life with different medications, sometimes incorrect, sometimes overly sedating
   b. Often compares himself to people with other diagnosis' he is lumped together with
   c. He was never a part of the conversation about treatment, but things improved when he was able to write his own behavior plan in high school as a senior
   d. Misdiagnosis—like they're trying to pathologize his behaviors
   e. Understanding his actions, behaviors and thoughts in the frame of his diagnosis
B. Sense of not belonging
   a. Outpatient/hospitals: usually had a different diagnosis than other members there
      i. Others who had "psychotic symptoms"
      ii. Criminals
      iii. "Severely behaviorally handicapped"
   b. Forced to participate in group activities at hospitals and Buckeye Ranch, even though he preferred to be on his own
   c. Generational differences between peers in college classes and others in hospitals
   d. Teased for being "different" throughout middle school and high school
   e. Two years of rejection from Deaf peers until acceptance (felt hopeless)
   f. Meet-up groups/dating: suicidal in 2017
C. Communication: Prefers sign language
   a. College certification
   b. Felt he fit in more with deaf community
   c. How he communicated versus what he communicated about (childhood resentment)
   d. Difficulty socializing, found it easier to socialize via sign language
   e. Prefers jobs for which not a lot of communication is necessary

        i. Current job: at first preferred to only speak with supervisor, now sometimes speaks to other colleagues
     f. Colleagues cussing at work causes confusion for him
  D. Empowered
     a. Taught himself sign language
     b. Taught himself how to ride public transportation
     c. Described disclosing diagnosis to current employer as "weight lifted"
     d. Living on own: found role model in Grandma and modeled living style after her
     e. Seeking employment to gain status and help with relationships
     f. Budgeting
  E. Childhood resentment
     a. Lots of anger, this comes up a lot
     b. "I did not feel loved" by parents
        i. Parents doing their best based on clinical recommendations
     c. Dad's mindset of disability isn't real
     d. Verbal and physical abuse by parents
     e. In school "I got all the blame"
  F. Mental health
     a. Depression, feelings of isolation, suicidal
     b. Feeling misunderstood
     c. Understanding his own experiences through the lens of autism diagnosis (anger, sensory overload, loud noises effect job performance)
     d. Email to current boss and disclosure of Autism diagnosis at work (described disclosing diagnosis to current employer as "weight lifted")
  G. Seeking companionship
     a. Snuggle buddies
     b. Need for touch
     c. Sometimes people have misunderstandings when told about his ASD

d. Taking another person's words literally sometimes interferes with his relationships (romantic, friends, and coworkers)

Axial Coding

Axial coding is largely a transitional cycle between initial coding and theoretical coding; it determines which codes are dominant or less important and links categories with subcategories to assess how they relate. During axial coding, the researcher takes codes or categories from initial or focused coding and defines properties and dimensions before categorization (Strauss & Corbin, 1998). Axial coding allows researchers to think through causation suggested by data, which is necessary for grounded theory analysis and includes the following elements: (a) *contexts*—settings and boundaries where action and process occur; (b) *conditions*—routines and situations that do or do not occur in the contexts; (c) *interactions*—specific types, qualities, and strategies of exchange between people in these contexts and conditions; and (d) *consequence*— outcomes and results of these contexts, conditions, and interactions (Saldaña, 2016). Results of my axial coding process led to the following restructuring of categories and subcategories:

A. Isolation
   a. Childhood Resentment
      i. Parents Doing Their Best Based on Clinical Recommendations
   b. Mental Health
   c. Seeking Companionship
   d. Sense of Not Belonging
   e. Diagnosis and Treatment
B. Empowerment

   a. Communication: Sign Language
   b. Living on Own
   c. Employment
   d. Self-Autonomous

Theoretical (Selective) Coding

Theoretical coding helps with discovery of core or central categories identifying primary themes of the research. Core or central category refers to the primary theme of the research and identifies the major conflict, obstacle, problem, issue, or concern facing participants. Saldaña (2016) noted, "All categories and concepts become systematically integrated around the central/core category that suggests a theoretical explanation for the phenomenon" (p. 250). It is not the theory itself but instead keywords which trigger discussion about theory and specifies possible relationships between categories, thus facilitating the move from analysis to theory. The theory can be new, or it can elaborate on a previous theory. The theory states what, how, and why something happens and includes the following elements: (a) predicts and controls action through logic spanning if–then, when–then, and because–that's why constructions; (b) accounts for variation in empirical observations; (c) explains how or why something happens by stating its cause(s) and outcome(s); and (d) provides insights and guidance for improving social life (Charmz, 2012; Saldaña, 2016). Data analysis from Adam's story, combined with analysis from selected autobiographies, led to two theories, which are discussed in detail in Part Three.

Constant Comparison Model

Charmaz (2012) stated, "Through comparing data with data, we learn what our research participants view as problematic and begin to treat it analytically" (p. 116). Comparing Adam's experiences with those of other adults on the spectrum allowed me to think about these collective experiences through an analytical lens. Charmaz referred to this method of constant comparison as coding incident with incident. During my analysis, I compared contexts between Adam and the autobiography authors; even if contexts were similar, specific experiences were sometimes different. For example, the name of a code might be the same, but specific experiences contextualizing that code may have been different among various people. The constant comparison model allowed me to define properties of my codes and use specific examples from different participants, which led to comparative patterns across authors and contrasts to Adam's experiences. Charmaz (2012) further explained, "Grounded theorists use this method to reveal the properties and range of the emergent categories and raise level of abstraction of their developing analysis" (p. 342).

There were 13 themes developed from the 20 autobiographies, which are listed below. Part Two went deeper into themes deemed most prevalent among the autobiographies and Adam's story. While some autobiographies were written in chronological order of the author's lives, many were not written chronologically, but rather presented as passages of various experiences, sometimes broken into themes that were important to the authors, and sometimes broken into categories such as employment or schooling experiences. To this end, we presented Adam's story as themes, many of which overlapped with the themes derived from the autobiographies. Themes materializing from the autobiographies were:

- Mental Health
- Medical Treatment
- Influence of Parents
- Isolation
- Empowerment
- Understanding One's Own Experiences Through an ASD Diagnosis
- Sensory Experiences
- Employment: Differences in Neurodivergent Needs
- Education: Differences in Needs
- Friendship
- Family Life Experiences (marriage/dating/children)
- Societal Expectations
- Sexual Abuse

The combination of the analysis of Adam's story with the constant comparison method used with the autobiographies is explained in detail in Part Three.

Researcher Positionality

When conducting qualitative research, it is important to note the role of the researcher as a research instrument (Xu & Storr, 2012). Charmaz (2012) affirmed, "If we start with the assumption that social reality is multiple, processual, and constructed, then we must take the researcher's position, privileges, perspectives, and interactions into account as an inherent part of the research reality" (p. 13). In other words, it is important to accept researchers are not neutral observers nor value free, and researchers' construction and interpretation of data will influence data analysis. What Xu and Storr (2012) and Charmaz (2012) emphasized is my life experiences, both personal and professional, played a role in shaping the direction of this study and the construction and interpretation of the results. To maintain transparency and show how our different life experiences may have influenced our respective contributions to this research, I have disclosed background information about myself and Adam, describing our circumstances at the time this study was conducted in addition to past experiences that shaped our circumstances.

Adam is a white male in his late-30s. He grew up with his parents and sister in Ohio and was diagnosed with Asperger's Syndrome at age 12. According to DSM-IV (1994), which is what was used when Adam was diagnosed, Asperger's Syndrome was a form of ASD that included impairments in social and communication functions, but no delays in cognitive development. There was limited understanding of ASD when Adam was diagnosed, and in addition to years of therapy, he spent several years living in various institutions and facilities.

Adam currently lives by himself in a trailer in Santa Ana, California. He prefers to live alone and enjoys living in the trailer park. Adam attended Cincinnati State College and earned a certificate in Deaf Studies because he enjoys communicating in sign language. While growing up, Adam had a tumultuous relationship with his parents; he felt they did not understand him, nor did they provide the kind of support he needed. Adam currently has a more amicable relationship with his parents. Adam has also found it difficult to make and keep friends. One reason he decided to learn sign language was because he felt more comfortable communicating via sign language than through verbal means. I do not know sign language, so although Adam is now far more comfortable speaking verbally, I am an outsider to his preferred communication style.

I am a 32-year-old female of Indian descent who was born and raised in southern California. Though I do not have a diagnosis of ASD, I have been diagnosed with Generalized Anxiety Disorder and have regularly attended cognitive-behavioral therapy with a psychologist for the last 12 years. I have always had a positive relationship with my parents, who have been supportive of my professional and personal endeavors. My bachelor's and master's degrees are in psychology, I am a board-certified behavior analyst, and I am currently enrolled in a Ph.D. program in education and disability studies. I am cognizant Adam may perceive a power dynamic, as I am a behavior analyst and often work with autistic individuals. To offset any perceived power dynamic, I worked diligently to foster a collaborative environment in which Adam and I could approach this research project as coauthors. Because I do not have previous book-writing experience, Adam and I have continued to navigate the process together. I am also married and have one child. Although Adam is not in a relationship, dating is often a topic of discussion and he enrolls services of a professional cuddler when he has sufficient financial resources.

Any research involving another person's story faces an ethical conundrum. On one hand, I wanted to provide a platform for Adam to share his story in his own words, as it would allow him to "relive, control, transform, (re-) imagine events, to reclaim and construct chosen identities, social interactions and communities" (Gready, 2013, p. 240). I must also note the nature of personal stories and memories is not static, but rather a dynamic interaction between myself and Adam. As Tamboukou et al. (2013) explained, narrative, "experience-centered research stresses that such representations vary drastically over time, and across the circumstances within which one lives, so that a single phenomenon may produce very different stories, even from the same person" (p. 6). For example, there was no way for me to know parts of Adam's story I did not ask about because Adam preferred I ask him questions to which he could respond. Furthermore, when anyone shares memories, it is natural to tell different parts of a story based on the person to whom you are speaking (Tamboukou et al., 2013). Although Adam may have told me parts of his story based on questions I asked him, he may recount different aspects of his story when speaking to a family member or friend. Additionally, many research participants who share their stories do not have any control of how their stories are interpreted or shared (Gready, 2013). Though there is no solution per se, I acknowledge I played a role in shaping Adam's story and have remained transparent on how we tried to mitigate this issue as much as possible.

Earlier in this chapter, I outlined many of the tools we used to engage in meaningful and trustworthy qualitative research. These tools included asking Adam to member check, including Adam as a coauthor and coresearcher rather than a research participant, and asking open-ended and follow-up questions based on what he told me, rather than having a list of planned questions. I also shared my thematic analysis with Adam and will publish his story as a book so his voice can reach a wider audience. Finally, I updated Adam every step of the study. In this qualitative research—especially when sharing another person's story—it is imperative to reflect on how my background affected our communication, influenced the shaping of Adam's story, and how this research experience with Adam has changed me as a researcher.

For example, in professional research I had conducted before beginning this study with Adam, I had identified employment, college, independent living, and relationships as four main themes of adulthood. When I first started having conversations with Adam, my questions typically reflected these four themes. As I heard more of Adam's story, however, I learned there were far more themes to be recognized. In fact, these four themes were not actually themes; rather, they were settings where additional themes emerged, such as isolation and empowerment. Moreover, although my research started out to encapsulate the experiences of autistic adults, I realized when talking to Adam his childhood experiences impacted many of his adulthood experiences. Subsequently, my questions shifted from topics such as, "tell me about your first job" and "what was it like to live on your own" to much more general questions such as, "tell me about your childhood" and "what is your first memory?" With these questions I was able to delve deeper into Adam's experiences and understand how those experiences have continued to impact his endeavors.

Conclusion

Chase (2012) described narrative inquiry as "meaning making through the shaping or ordering of experience, a way of understanding one's own or others' actions, of organizing events and objects into a meaningful whole, of connecting and seeing the consequences of actions and events over time" (p. 56). Rather than imposing an academic agenda on Adam or observing him without his input, Adam and I used concepts of narrative inquiry to cocreate our research questions and purpose of our research through dialogue. As per DS framework, Adam was seen as the expert on autism, whereas my expertise emerged when assisting Adam as he articulated his story on his terms. Using narrative inquiry provided a way to make sense of the studied world—in this case, Adam's world, and by extension, the worlds of others on the autism spectrum—to gain a better understanding of their experiences. Ultimately, my goal is to use this information to advocate for modified behavior toward autistic people and to create more inclusive and accepting environments, rather than imposing preconceived notions of appropriate social behavior onto others.

Grounded theory analysis was selected for this research project because it complements the constructionist, ontological, and epistemological frames of DS and narrative inquiry.

Therapists can create training programs for employers, teachers, and other therapists rather than solely focusing on training programs for autistic people. By shifting focus to learning from study participants, we used narrative inquiry methodology and a DS framework to develop a socially just form of research methodology. This contrasts with traditional academic research, which may oppress research participants by assuming a position of power in favor of the researchers.

Grounded theory analysis allowed me to construct codes rather than use preconceived categories, and constant interaction with the data during my analysis led me to theoretical frameworks not often cited in mainstream educational research. The neurodiversity paradigm and the theory of monotropism will help clinicians and researchers better understand behavioral patterns of individuals with ASD. These theoretical frameworks are discussed in Part Three and provide insights into patterns of behavior and thinking in the autism community, with an emphasis on the substantial variation of autistic experiences. These two frameworks can guide us all toward modifying our own behaviors and creating a more accepting and understanding society.

Part Two

Redefining Experts: Adam's Story
Coauthor: Adam Paul Valerius

Adam's story is presented in the following chapters. Because many themes I found were present throughout his lifetime, his life story is presented chronologically, and emergent themes are further analyzed in Part Three. Certain sentences are bolded to reflect particularly strong sentiments from Adam. Some names and places of businesses were reduced to their first letter to protect privacy. Adam and I are listed as coauthors of this book to emphasize his role as coresearcher and equal contributor to this body of research.

Chapter Three

Childhood Memories

I say my childhood was 80 % bad and 20 % good. Growing up, my parents were verbally abusive, but the only physical abuse was from my dad, at least 3 times a week until my teenage years. He would spank me for the pettiest reasons. It'll always be upsetting to think about. **I prefer to remember positive childhood memories, but there are some negative ones that have shaped me and my relationship with my parents.**

I have one sister and no brothers. We are close. When we were younger, when the weather was nice, we would just take a recreational bike ride on the route that I had mapped out for us in the neighborhood. It was a pretty long ride, like 4 miles round trip. My sister got abused a lot less than me because I think she cared a lot more about how she made my parents feel, and I didn't. I began to view my father as my enemy when I was about 3 months out from turning seven. He believed that the 6-year-old I was at the time would automatically know the difference between truth telling and lying and when he decided to accuse me of lying, he spanked me. The date was Wednesday, August 1, 1990, and the time of day was 2:38 p.m. I told him I hated him, like any 7-year-old does, and I ran upstairs to my room and cried.

I started having outbursts at around the age of 7, so when I was 10 years old, my parents decided to take me to the doctor. By the time I was 12, my parents, my doctors, and I were pretty convinced that I didn't have a disability. The doctors were throwing 1970s adages at me like, "if you always do what you always did, you'll always get what you always got." It made no sense to me.

During the first quarter of 1994, my mother said she would kill me because the dog ran away, and I actually took it literally. When my mother said that, I just reacted full blast, but then after she started calming down, I remarked that I'm still alive. I think she probably understands now that I took her statement literally, but she definitely did not fully understand then. I think she probably went behind my back and told some doctors about my outburst.

On March 31, 1996, when I was 12 years old, I had a particularly severe outburst, so my parents decided to put me in the psychiatric ward in Cincinnati Children's Hospital Medical Center (CCHMC). My father manhandled me into the car. I knew where I was going, and I did not want to go. I was very confused when I got there. I was there for 2 weeks and on Friday, April 12, 1996, I got my diagnosis of Asperger Syndrome from a psychiatrist who worked there.

While I was there, I was required to participate in a lot of group activities that I really did not want to do. **Prior to the hospitalization I was happy just being a loner, but in the hospital, that was not acceptable**. The day would start with the goals group with about 10 people, and I always struggled to make an acceptable goal. The nurses decided what was acceptable. I had one roommate, who was younger than me. The other children in the ward had bipolar disorder, schizophrenia, or spoke about hearing voices. I did not feel like I could relate to them at all because I did not have similar symptoms and had nothing in common with the other kids. I really hated it and wanted to get out of there.

Over the 2 weeks in the hospital my parents came to visit me at least eight times. Most of those visits were full of tension because they still wanted me in the hospital, and I didn't want to be there. The doctors said I won't be safe if I go home, but I disagreed. I do not know what changed in the 2 weeks and why I was allowed to go home.

CHILDHOOD MEMORIES

Growing up I felt different, but I didn't know I was medically different until that hospitalization. About a month after I was home from the hospital, I found a bunch of books about Asperger Syndrome on the dining table, and I asked my mother why we had those books. She told me that was my diagnosis. After my mother finished reading the books, I read a couple of the books. I feel like the descriptions of Asperger Syndrome sounded like me, it was a very well-fitting description. For most of my life I thought that my first and only autism diagnosis was Asperger Syndrome, but well into my adulthood, my mother informed me that a pediatrician had diagnosed me with Pervasive Developmental Disorder-Not Otherwise Specified (PDD-NOS) when I was 3.

I had no initial emotional reaction to my diagnosis. **During my childhood, my father held a mindset that there is no such thing as a disability, and all who claim to have one are "just not trying."** Despite his mindset, **my diagnosis immediately helped me understand** why I got angrier than most people get when yelled at. It also helped me understand why I was such a picky eater and had intolerances for things like the visual appearance of the vertical slots of the speaker grille on a toy guitar amp, the taste of most cheeses, and the tactile feel of the non-slip mats on the stairs of a waterpark ride (of course I was standing on it barefoot while lugging a HEAVY sled for use on that particular slide).

I received the diagnoses of Psychotic Disorder NOS and Asperger Syndrome at the same time, the conclusion of my first-ever psychiatric hospitalization on Friday, April 12, 1996. I only agree with Asperger's and NOT Psychotic Disorder NOS. I believe the thought processes they claimed were "delusions" were actually caused by the brain malformation we later discovered when my then-psychiatrist ordered an MRI in 2001, 5 years after they said I was "delusional." In diagnosing me psychotic, they did claim hallucinations, but mostly focused on delusions to justify their mistreatment of me. The "hallucinations" they claimed were my confusion of my thoughts manifesting as spoken words that seemed to stop when I saw the battery being removed from our 1987 First Alert smoke detector. They took this as "Adam thinks a 1987 smoke detector is talking to him when it can't." My mother once went as far as claiming I hallucinated my father's voice in places he wasn't physically present with me. Again, wrong, because I was voluntarily imagining a conversation with him that I thought was coming but didn't actually come. They just called their every disagreement with me another "delusion" and threatened force if I didn't voluntarily take larger and larger pills that sedated me more and more (the pills weren't physically larger; they just contained higher and higher numbers of milligrams of the medications).

During my clozapine withdrawal in 2005, doctors said I was experiencing "paranoid delusions." I associate those thought processes with the withdrawal and not an actual psychotic disorder. The withdrawal has since stopped, and I have not taken any antipsychotic medications whatsoever in almost 11 years. As Sneha has observed me for the past 5 of these 11 years, she knows I'm FINE. I do wish the doctors in Cincinnati had agreed to give me an antidote for the withdrawal instead of telling me to just get back on the very medication I'm withdrawing from, which I never agreed to do except under duress when I was civilly committed.

I was started on an antidepressant drug at the age of 12, but the doctors changed the medication when I was in the hospital to an antipsychotic drug. I felt worse being on any of the medications than I did without the medications. The antipsychotic was heavily sedating for me, which made it hard for me to get through the day. These antipsychotic drugs were being used off label for me, which means it was not being used as the pharmaceutical company's intended use. The doctors prescribed it to me because they thought it would "take the edge off," but really, antipsychotic medications are meant to suppress delusions and hallucinations, which I did not have and have never had. They kept changing up the exact medication, but each of the medicines only helped me feel 10 % calmer.

Beginning in elementary school, I had classroom aides within my general education classroom, but I do not remember what they did for or with me. The aides may have been there for me, but I thought they were there for other kids.

I began teaching myself sign language in 1997 upon becoming aware that mainstreamed Deaf kids were attending my school. I always hated being sociable in environments where everyone is shouting over the top of everyone else. My middle school's lunchroom was certainly like that every day, and so were all of my extended family gatherings. After feeling like I could not fit in with the verbal majority I decided to see if I could fit in with the Deaf kids. Initially, I did not, but after nearly 2 years of rejection I finally did.

The first book I purchased to teach myself sign language was The Pocket Dictionary of Signing. *Most of the directions on how to make the signs were clear, but considering currently available technologies, I would highly recommend against my method. I did not become fluent until 1999, and still did not have a full vocabulary in sign language until 2003.*

Leading up to my first-ever psychiatric hospitalization in 1996, I felt that I couldn't have friends . . . that was, until I discovered I was going to school with Deaf kids who were being mainstreamed. I then decided to learn sign [language] to connect with them and see if I really couldn't have friends. Turns out I can, in fact, have friends.

I have dealt with service providers in Hamilton County Developmental Disabilities Services who I felt did not listen attentively and wished I could have been signing with them. The final service facilitator I had with them prior to permanently leaving their service area actually did have signing skills which he used with me when we were physically present with each other.

It was cathartic for me to talk about these childhood experiences with Sneha and with others who won't just defend my parents and who won't just defend everyone who was mistreating me. I want this book out because it's less likely to be ignored than an online post. What if I just go online, and I just write all this stuff on social media? Very few people are gonna bother to look at it. I've already tried that. Over the years, it hasn't worked. Publishing a book will make my story my legitimate.

Chapter Four

Adolescence

My outbursts got worse throughout my adolescence, and within the year 1999 I was hospitalized three times, for about 2 weeks each time. I was 15 years old then. **While I was in the hospital, I felt isolated in public. There were people around me, but I had nothing in common with them, so I refused to interact with them. I trusted my parents a lot less because they kept hospitalizing me.**

In the year 2000, when I was 16 years old, I was placed in long-term care in a facility called The Buckeye Ranch in Ohio. My parents told me in February, and I was very angry that I was still going to be put in a place where I would be locked up. My parents were following the recommendations of the psychiatrist of CCHMC. They told me that I would stay there until the doctor there told me I was ready to go home. **The gruffness of the staff there made it feel like a jail-like environment; they raised their voices and talked down to us.** When I first got there I had a roommate, but as my stay progressed and my privilege level rose, I was given a room by myself. **The rooms felt like a jail cell.** There was no covering on the window and I was forbidden from closing the door. It was a small room with just a bed and small desk. Bathrooms were shared with two other people.

Within the locked area there were four units, and the open campus ranch had an additional five units. I was in the locked unit of the intensive care center (ICC). Each unit of the ICC had eight students, so a total of 32 students in the locked units, and the open campus had another 40. I mostly interacted with the eight people in my unit plus the staff. **I was there for 94 days. At least they customized a program for me, unlike the hospital, but I feel that my stay there benefitted me very little.** For the first 3 weeks I had to be at the ranch 24/7, but then I was allowed to go home on the weekends.

At the ranch, we had to do similar activities as we did in the psychiatric ward at the hospitals. We started the day with goal groups in the morning and had school classes on the weekdays. **Again, I did not feel like anyone there was similar to me.** The others there seemed to have more severe psychotic symptoms than those I met in the hospital, and I never had psychotic symptoms to begin with. I did not make any friends there. **Once the staff became aware of my sign language skills, they allowed me to socialize with the deaf kids, who were in another unit.** I enjoyed socializing with them because I felt that I had better communication with them.

My parents came and took me home every weekend. I was nervous about going home because I was resentful about my placement at the ranch, but I was relieved to be home, all at the same time. Almost immediately after I went home from the ranch, I was making slip ups in conversations that resulted in shouting matches with my parents. An example is I mentioned getting the hell out of my parents' house and they really did not like that.

For the first month of the following school year after I left the ranch, **I was sent to a school that was for students considered severely, behaviorally handicapped.** We hoped it would work out better than it did. I was the only student at the school who did not have a probation officer. **Again, I did not belong there.** My parents decided to pull me out of there because every student in the school was a criminal except for me. I was then homeschooled for a month of my final year of high school.

When I first started meeting the Deaf kids at my school, I didn't feel that I fit in with them because I thought signing was supposed to be slower than speech, and it isn't. After nearly 2 years of rejection because I wasn't able to follow their fluent signing, I recalled a short exchange between me and the first of the Deaf kids I met in the earliest months of me being a signer:

> Jhumur: Where's Lori? (signing Lori's sign name that I didn't recognize)
> Me: What does L with thumb touching breast mean?
> Jhumur: L-O-R-I.
> Me: I don't-know.

I honestly didn't know that one of the girl's names was Lori, nor did I know where this Lori was at that moment. In ASL, when you ask where someone is, it's acceptable and often expected that you actually omit the sign for 'where' and just sign the person's sign name with furrowed eyebrows which is the facial expression for an open-ended question. I did not learn this until 2001, when I took my first formal ASL class at Cincinnati State College. So, I emailed one of the Deaf boys and told him he could clarify himself to me in a similar manner. I can just show him the sign I didn't understand and ask him to spell out what it means, especially if it was someone's sign name that I didn't happen to know. The next day at lunch, he was trying to shout my name over the din in the lunch room and I didn't hear him until the third time which was more distorted than the first two times. Once I went over to where he was:

> Me: Did you get my email last night? Brendan: Yes.
> Me: Does this mean we are friends again? Brendan: Yes. [gave me high-five]

Two weeks later, Allen, the best of my Deaf friends at Finneytown High School found out about my attempts to connect with them and accepted me more than any of the others did. We remained friends for nearly 20 years until I decided to #DeleteFacebook on April 21, 2018.

From 2003 until 2012, I was so much more comfortable communicating in sign language because it does not require extra force in sending a message like speech does in loud environments or at far distances from the listener. I love those facts about sign language! In

Cincinnati I perceived a bias against it in most of the people there. In Orange County, California, I perceive an even stronger bias against it because most Deaf people in Cincinnati are mute and most Deaf people in Orange County are not. The Deaf of SoCal feel a need to develop speaking voices because society doesn't want them signing except amongst each other. Their speaking voices often cause sensory overload for autistic folks because they cannot hear how loud they are.

I remember that, beginning in high school, I had a resource bell, which means that I spent a whole class period in the resource room. I was required to do some activities that I did not feel were relevant, like word searches and cryptograms. There were approximately eight other students in the class, and they mostly had different mental illnesses such as schizophrenia and bipolar disorder. I know this because I was told by the teacher and my parents, who also told me that the class was for Severely Behaviorally Handicapped (SBH) students. **I felt that I did not belong in that class, but I was in the class all throughout high school and I do not think it benefitted me at all.**

I had Individualized Education Programs (IEP) since elementary school, which I did not know until high school. **I was never a part of any IEPs until the very end, in my senior year of high school.** They finally started inviting me to join the IEP meetings after I came back from Buckeye Ranch during my senior year. Although I was a part of the meeting, I had very little say in my behavioral and treatment goals. **I wish they had asked my opinion instead of it feeling like it was them versus me.**

I wrote up a behavior contract to convince the board of education, who had expelled me from my high school before I was sent to the ranch, to let me back in. It was my idea to write up the behavior contract. I had been expelled from my high school for fleeing the campus several times. **I fled the campus because I was too upset to function in class because I was being tormented by other students.** They teased me and were mean to me my entire time in high school and middle school. I would go home because I lived near the school. I would tell the teacher first, then they would send me to the principal's office, where **they would tell me to just calm down and deal with it, which I could not do. I got all the blame every time.**

My high school decided to let me back in to resume attending school and graduate with my class. At the end of that school year I graduated. **I did not run away again because they agreed with what I wrote in the behavior contract**, that if I was too upset to be in class I would go to the attendance office and call my mother. That happened at least half a dozen times, and my mother would come pick me up and take me home, and I did not get in trouble for that.

When I graduated from high school I still lived with my parents for another 5 months. I then moved to a group home 15 miles south of my parents' house; it was still about 10 miles to my college. I didn't really want to go to the group home, but I wasn't really getting along with my parents and I was qualified for developmental disability services in Ohio, so they paid for the group home. My mother had me screened for eligibility, I don't remember how she made the decision to have this screening happen. My service coordinator then drove me past the group home and told me that if things get too bad between me and my parents, I could move there. My service coordinator knew that I was having a tough time with my parents because I vented to her; I had to vent to someone in between my therapy sessions. I would see her two to three times a week, we would go out to eat and she would let me talk about anything I wanted to in relation to how I was doing, my experiences with college, and my parents. I trusted her and felt that I could open up to her somewhat, despite her believing my misdiagnosis of psychosis. I never could find a service coordinator who agreed with me that the diagnosis was not correct. The longer I knew her, the worse it got and the less I felt like I could talk to her, because she would just keep agreeing with the misdiagnosis and tell me that I need to take antipsychotic medication again, which I knew would not help.

My childhood was extremely traumatic due to frequent physical punishment from my father, frequent psychiatric hospitalizations, and frequent force used against me by psychiatric nurses. My parents and I were all very angry at each other, and I couldn't wait to break away from them. I just needed a few more months to wait for my Supplemental Security Income to start and to find a place I could afford with it. But on my paternal grandmother's 80th birthday, which was 20 days after my 18th birthday, my father threatened to call the police for trespassing charges if I was not off "his property" by the time he arrived home from work. Subfreezing temperatures were definitely occurring that day in Cincinnati. My parents both vehemently deny this threat was ever said, but I often remember things people say for YEARS after they forget!

When my father first threatened trespassing charges, I didn't have another home or any money to pay for that other home. This was my final moment of living with them. I felt that he no longer cared if I had a roof over my head. Knowing that I had the option to move to the group home, I ran as fast as I could to the nearest Cincinnati Metro Bus stop, where I called my service coordinator and told her what happened. She arranged for me to move into the group home within a few hours. Then I caught the bus and I went to my therapist because it was my regular scheduled appointment for that week. My mom picked me up from my therapist's office, and she had packed some of my stuff. The owner of the group home called me when I was in the car, offering that I move into the group home and I responded by saying, "yes please, I am homeless." Once I got off the phone, my mother yelled at me, denying I was homeless. I became very disrespectful and said, "excuse me ma'am, your husband just kicked me off his property. You don't even own that place." I don't even remember the rest of the conversation because we were both so angry. **She didn't really owe me anything, but she was trying to help because she still cared about me,** even though, ultimately, she chose her husband over me. Then she dropped me at the group home, where I moved in that day, December 11, 2001.

I walked through the doors and there was a brief conversation between myself, my mom, and the owner of the group home. The owner took me to my room; it was my own room. **I got out my laptop and just started typing out all my frustrations.** I ate the dinner that was cooked by the group home operators, and it really didn't taste all that good. I immediately missed my father's cooking. I met most of the other people that lived there the next day. **I tried not to talk to them because I had always been a recluse for my whole life up to that point, aside from my efforts to socialize with the signing community.** I associate my reclusive ways with my condition of

Autism. I was scared that they weren't going to accept me because I had only been there a month when the group operator started cussing at me, saying, "if you don't like the rules, get the f-bomb out." I think it was actually directed at someone else but because I come from a Catholic family, I was raised to have a bias against all profanity, which I have since lost. At the group home I would listen to music or work on my college homework. The other group home members were older (40s) and were not really nice. They were snappy all the time and verbally abusive toward me, each other, and everyone who came in the house. Five of us lived there at the time. I spent a lot of time there because I had nowhere else to go. I was nowhere ready to work at the time. The group home was funded in full by Hamilton County Board of Developmental Disabilities Services because I was waiting for my SSI to start.

I spoke to my parents at least three times a week. The first conversation was 72 hours after I moved to the group home. My father said he regretted kicking me out, but he refused to reverse his decision. **I did not feel loved, and I did not talk a lot to him because I was angry.** I was a lot less angry with my mother, but I didn't speak to her much more than I spoke to my dad because she forces dad on me, and I just wanted to shun him. I saw my dad every week for each of those 3 months because I would take the bus to college, but the bus stopped running while I was there, so my dad would pick me up and drop me to the group home. I really didn't talk to him, I just listened to recorded music, and he didn't try to talk to me much, either. I would see my mom about twice a month. I went back to my parents' house for Christmas and spent the night there, which was okay, but I wish they would have let me move back in until my SSI started. I was at the group home for a total of 3 months and then I moved to my first apartment on March 9, 2002.

Outside of school I started to have psychological counseling right before my 18th birthday. I didn't ask for it, but a psychiatrist my parents made me see decided that I needed counseling. I saw this therapist weekly for about 3 years. It wasn't really helpful because I wasn't ready to make any changes at that time.

I have gone to family therapy in the past, but it's mostly been a suggestion from others who previously knew me. I think they noticed in my early adulthood that my resentment of how I was raised was growing, especially once I stopped taking my medication and suffered some severe withdrawal symptoms. These withdrawal symptoms caused me to wreck the only motor vehicle I ever owned three times, and abandon my apartment thinking that I could just sell my car and get the money for an airline ticket to move to Seattle, Washington. That didn't work because I realized my car would not actually sell for the amount I needed for the airline ticket.

I was in my early 20s the last time we talked about going back to family therapy. My mother said it's nothing but a source of stress and arguments for all three of us, which I agree is an accurate description of how our family therapy was. My parents and I went to family therapy with the clinician at the Buckeye Ranch psychiatric institution. They never agreed with me and they always made it very clear that they are right and I am wrong. That they are the plaintiffs and I am the defendant, and this is a criminal case. I was even threatened with the second-most severe punishment doled out at the ranch, which I had already previously received after an unrelated incident 2 months prior.

> Much earlier in my life we had family therapy approximately every 2 or 3 weeks with Dr.

Boyles; he was located less than a mile from the house where I grew up. Those sessions were much calmer although Dr. Boyles frequently used metaphors and adages that were popular in the 1970s and I could not comprehend them.

I did talk about the childhood abuse in the family therapy sessions but they discredited me. My parents, plus the family therapist, everyone discredited me. I suggested going back to family therapy when I was in my 20s based on suggestions from my high school classmate plus suggestions from therapists I was seeing at that time. I thought it would help. I was disappointed when they didn't agree to go to family therapy. Nowadays, I just think I just have to accept that they're going to just sweep everything under the rug. They're both in their 60s and I think they're just accepting that I will always keep the same perspective, I will maintain that they abused me no matter who discredits me or who wants to call me delusional or psychotic because of these allegations. Now there's only verbal abuse when talking about certain issues.

Chapter Five

Transitioning to Adulthood

In 2001, I graduated from Finneytown High School in the suburbs of Cincinnati, Ohio. When I was in high school I didn't have any goals for the future, I just wanted high school to be over with! However, during my senior year I had my mother look into some college courses that I could take on American Sign Language at a college that was inexpensive and within walking distance of the Cincinnati Metro bus lines. We found Cincinnati State College, and I began taking classes in April 2001, shortly before I graduated from high school. **My original plan was to never go to college, but I was very interested in sign language and I enjoyed learning more about it.** I took 3 years' worth of sign language classes at this college. I majored in Deaf Studies and earned a certificate in Deaf Studies. I earned this certificate for the personal satisfaction and knowledge of sign language. I did not take classes in any other subjects.

College Experiences

To get to and from college, I rode the Cincinnati Metro buses. I began teaching myself how to ride public mass transit buses about 2 months before my 18th birthday. I didn't want to rely on my parents like they were my taxi or something. I had a temporary driver's license, but became extremely nervous every time I practiced driving my father's old 1990 Geo Prizm base model. So, I contacted Cincinnati Metro to find out which routes I needed to go from the house where I grew up to my therapist's office and attempted to travel there alone on the buses. I did well from the first attempt forward. There was one time, however, when I mistakenly crossed the street when I was supposed to catch the bus on the same side of the street where I already was, and I ended up in a very dangerous neighborhood. The bus took me back into Downtown Cincinnati soon thereafter and no one threatened me.

Around my 20th birthday, I paid $360 to Driver's Ed Academy in Cincinnati to have a driving instructor come over with a driver's ed car and give me the chance to try to get comfortable driving. Driver's ed cars are equipped with a second brake pedal on the passenger side so that the instructor can stop the car if I couldn't stop in time. Five lessons cost $300, and the extra $60 was to borrow the driver's ed car in which to take my driving test. Once I got comfortable around the end of the second lesson, I used the remaining lessons to learn the rest of what I needed to know for my test, and then was tested by the hardest examiner in the whole exam station. He passed me on my first try, and I was issued an unrestricted driver's license in December of 2003. **My parents were very proud of me** for learning how to drive. In 2004, about a month before my 21st birthday, I bought my mother's old 1994 Geo Prizm LSI from her for $500. I drove it until February of 2005, when a medication withdrawal left me with severe insomnia and I could no longer drive safely. I was sad, I wish I hadn't had to stop driving.

I never really got that close to any of my classmates in college. Most of them were two to three times my age, even older than my parents. I did have one classmate by whom I felt understood and exchanged weekly emails in between classes, and we continued to email after we graduated. She was also studying to earn her certificate in Deaf Studies.

We would sometimes chat for a few minutes before class. I did not enjoy chatting with her in person, but I enjoyed emailing with her. At the time I was making a lot more excuses about not comprehending nonverbal cues, which made it difficult for me to talk in person. She knew that because I had opened up to her a few months after we began emailing each other. I had explained my symptoms at the time, and she seemed to understand the difficulties I had to deal with.

Going into college I had decided that I would share my symptoms with anyone I spoke to. I would bring it up in conversations with classmates, teachers, and everyone, not caring what their reactions might be, or if it was relevant to the conversation. There was usually no initial reaction. **When my lack of social skills was most evident during certain incidents, their reactions were negative.** An example of such an incident was when, during class one day, break time was nearing, and I was already standing up. One classmate lectured me that it would be common sense to sit down until break time was actually called. I understood this as a generational conflict because many of my classmates were in their 40s–50s, and I was 19. I did not sit back down, and then I avoided her at break time. The reason I had stood up in the first place was that I was experiencing akathisia, which means it was hard for me to sit still, from an antipsychotic medicine I was taking at the time.

Getting people to understand my issues that are caused by Asperger Syndrome was challenging. I could tell that my teachers, colleagues, and especially the Dean of Humanities were very closed minded because of their responses when I would try to educate them about my condition. **I tried to educate them because I was being told that I was distracting other students, and I tried to explain why I could not help what I was doing that was considered distracting.** At the time, even I was confused, because I was oversedated from antipsychotic medications that I did not need. The behaviors included outbursts that consisted of me yelling, sometimes at the beginning of some of the labs that I had to take for my classes. I was probably just overwhelmed, especially when one of my classmates told me that the class was pissed at me. The students complained and then I was sternly lectured by the Dean of Humanities, and they threatened to call security on me if I attended the lab again, until they told me I could participate again. They asked me why I was yelling but I could not answer them because I was oversedated and I could not think straight. **When I tried to explain Asperger Syndrome to them, they did not care, and told me that I had to either stop the yelling or not attend the lab again.** I didn't attend the lab for two terms. I still was able to attend my other classes because I did not have the yelling behavior while in the other classes I was taking. Looking back now, I think that not getting along with certain people in that specific lab was what caused me to become overwhelmed, and the way I expressed that was by yelling.

I really didn't forge any friendships in college because after graduation most students got jobs and left the Cincinnati area. During college, I would just go to class and then go home. I do wish I could have made some friends, but it did not make sense given the age gap between me and the other students.

Whenever I was able to have a good lab without being overwhelmed and having an outburst, I consider Cincinnati State College a place where most of my good times happened after my 18th birthday. I was taking the program because I just wanted the personal satisfaction of the knowledge of American Sign Language and knowing an overview of the interpreting profession and American Deaf Culture. I had some good conversations with the lab coordinator during break times on topics ranging from Deaf culture to classes as well as personal experiences. I just never really had the right person to listen to me about my personal issues because the more I spoke about them, the more people felt alienated from me, and the less they wanted to hear about it anymore. **It made me feel hopeless, like, alright, this is me, I can't change, I'm pushing everyone away, I don't even mean to, I can't stop, so much for learning sign language to improve my communication skills.**

I would see my instructors outside of college when I would attend the Cincinnati-area deaf events, which were called silent dinners. My instructors would chat with me about people they've known for a while. I felt like I was connecting with my instructors on a different level, and it was interesting information. I also discovered who I could turn to for help if I was ever having communication issues.

I found the Cincinnati area Deaf events through my high school classmates who were deaf, when I was attending high school and college classes at the same time for 2 months. I went on my own because one of the silent dinners occurred at a mall that I had shopped at since I was a little boy, so I was comfortable because I already knew the mall and how to get to the food court area. I was very nervous because I wasn't really fluent in sign language yet and I had not really started college when I attended the first dinner. My first experience went well after I finished eating and delved into the socialization. **I made friends there, but those friends only lasted a few short months each because I think they just didn't understand Autism, and a lot of people were just not being clear with me that they were picking up on my childhood resentment.** It took me 10–15 years to realize that they were probably picking up on my resentment against my parents and childhood experiences, and they did not want to feel my resentment. I think this is because this was the main thing that I discussed with them. I think I talked about myself a bit too much and wish I had gotten to know them more than I did. I even had a therapist who said I talk a bit too much about myself. **My parents later told me that it was this therapist who encouraged them to be verbally abusive to me in my final 2 months of being 17, and this is why they treated me in that way.**

I continued going to these silent dinners all throughout college and for another 10 years.

I felt that I could communicate better with this population and felt more comfortable communicating in this way, although at times I would skip the dinners because I felt I was being shunned. I would sometimes try to start a conversation and not get a response.

I also discovered the Ohio Association of the Deaf-Blind and attended three out of four of their functions in 2003. I discovered them through one of my college instructors as well as another participant of the silent dinners. The first one I attended was more of a business conference, it was quite boring, but the other two were fun and allowed for social interactions via sign language. However, I again seemed to be talking about myself too much because my professor told me, "they don't want to feel my anger." The other participants did not say anything directly to me, but they must have told my instructor, because this particular instructor was not at one of the events on December 13, 2003. I **had to stop going to their events because in 2004, I was forbidden to attend any more events. I was told that certain members threatened to leave the group if I attended more events.** But they only told me that they were uncomfortable with me, **they didn't tell me why they were uncomfortable with me** or who was uncomfortable with me. I **was very depressed and hopeless** once again, because even though it is believed that autistic people never feel touch deprived, the Deaf-Blind read sign language by touching, so I did feel touch deprived for the first time in my life. **Then I spent 5 years trying to find another Deaf-Blind organization that would accept me, but I did not find one until I moved to Southern California.**

Employment

The year that I turned 18, I started actively seeking employment. I had a job developer through Ohio Valley Goodwill Industries who helped me with community job applications before I actually participated in their sheltered workshop the following year.

Due to my Asperger's I take every word I read to the most literal extreme and don't apply for most of the jobs I see because most employers exaggerate their requirements and I cannot be certain that I actually have the required skills and experience. I definitely don't have 2-plus years of experience with the latest versions of Microsoft Word and Excel! It would help if I had someone who actually understands these exaggerated job descriptions and has either assessed or been told what my skills and experiences are so that they can help me make an informed decision as to whether or not to apply for a particular job. But job developers who were available to me through the California Department of Rehabilitation (DoR) did not do that. They would just sit there and watch me apply for jobs, and in between our weekly appointments, expected me to apply for jobs completely on my own like people without disabilities do. What a poor excuse of help that was! I've had my case with DoR closed multiple times, and until their job developers offer to do more for me, I don't want my case reopened. Besides, I'd rather try to become able to apply for jobs completely on my own. My condition may always interfere with that, but I still want to try.

My first-ever job was being a grocery stocker at The Kroger Company's Finneytown store in the suburbs of Cincinnati, Ohio from 1999–2000. The job developer I had was present at the interview and prompted me, "tell the interviewer about this, tell the interviewer about that." That way I brought up what the interviewer wanted to hear and nothing else. Having my job developer there to prompt me was very helpful. **Most job interviews are tight molds for autistic people. We wiggle out of those molds, often unintentionally, and don't get the jobs because the interview is an extremely hard test of social skills that we can't help but fail.**

My main difficulty during this job was communicating with my direct supervisor, who I felt never seemed to listen attentively. I had to say nearly everything at least twice, which was extremely frustrating because I felt like I was not being heard. On my final day there, without being asked nor asking if it was okay, I decided to keep a written log of which products looked unsellable and would have to be returned to the stockroom. I thought I would be helping the company by doing so. Perhaps not. I also only drank a third of my can of soda, which I could not finish before my break ended, so I took it with me when I returned to work. My other supervisor shouted at the top of his lungs, "WHEN YOU ARE OUT IN THE AISLES, YOU CAN'T HAVE THAT!!!" I didn't understand what he was referring to—the written log, or the can of soda? The remainder of the conversation was nothing but an escalating shouting match that ended with me getting fired. I feel very strongly that I NEVER have to tolerate that kind of treatment from anyone other than a badged law enforcement officer. **I became angry, confused, overwhelmed and unable to figure out what to say or do.**

Now that I've matured and learned better coping skills, I would not yell back if I'm ever in a similar situation. I am also taking far less medication than I was taking at that time. Now I have learned that I can let my supervisors know beforehand that if I do something wrong, they should **break down the situation for me piece by piece so that I can properly understand what I did wrong, and how to do it correctly.** I will also let my supervisors know that if I am yelled at, I become overwhelmed and confused, and my first instinct will be to leave the situation; not because I do not care about the job, but I may not be able to respond in the moment.

I liked using my organizational skills in stocking the store shelves. I liked that I almost never had to communicate with anyone. I only recall being approached by a customer ONCE and was unable to help him find the item he was looking for since that item was not in the aisles I got assigned to stock. Like all my other community jobs between 1999 and 2001, I did not have a job coach accompanying me while I was at work. Perhaps a job coach could have helped by listening to my wordings and discussing them with me at break times so that I could improve them. Not knowing answers sometimes stresses me out. Talking while working really slows me down. I do not enjoy most of my social interactions, including during employment, and wish I could tightly limit them, but I fully acknowledge that is unrealistic.

In 2007, I had two more job developers through Jewish Vocational Services (JVS), which was also in Cincinnati, Ohio. They drove me to my skills assessments at Scholastic and Flexi, both of which only lasted a week. I really enjoyed both skills assessments. At Flexi, I was shipping pet accessories. I accomplished a greater quantity than expected once trained. I could not apply to work at Flexi because their workshop was located too far off the nearest bus line. At Scholastic, I don't remember what I was doing, but it was certainly something related to shipping and receiving. Scholastic is outside of Hamilton County, Ohio, where Cincinnati is, and I could not apply to work at Scholastic for the very same reason as Flexi. Many of the shipping and receiving jobs were full-time and at that time in my life I could only work part-time with my autism issues.

My first sheltered workshop was the Ohio Valley Goodwill Industries. I got into it by requesting the program through the Hamilton County Board of Developmental Disabilities Services (HCBDDS). I attended the program three times: in 2002, when I was 18, 2007, when

I was 23, and 2008–2009, when I was 24 and 25. A sheltered workshop is usually only available through developmental disabilities services systems. You do not have to go to an interview to get the job, but you do have to qualify for services.

My coworkers were much lower functioning than I am. They made noises that weren't exactly shrill but were certainly loud and repetitive, which made it difficult for me to complete my tasks. I felt that I was higher functioning than most of the coworkers, which made me feel like I did not belong there. Whenever there was no other work, I was "put on training" which was repeatedly counting the same pieces of hardware. **I often borrowed Trick Daddy's lyrics, saying, "I'm way too advanced for this!"**

Ohio Valley Goodwill Industries sends HCBDDS clients to work at two locations: Woodlawn and Westwood/Western Hills. I worked at Woodlawn in 2002 and 2007. In 2007 I could not get their van transportation service because I lived too far away. I took a cab every morning, which HCBDDS paid for. At the Woodlawn location, I enjoyed working the assembly line, which put together gift boxes for Babies "R" Us at the time. Most of the time I would be at the end of the assembly line, putting the lids on the boxes and stacking the completed items. **I liked that my tasks were very clear, and it gave me a sense of accomplishment to complete these tasks.**

Once the Westwood/Western Hills location opened, I worked there. I was able to take the bus to the work site. I taught myself how to ride the bus when I was 17. At the Westwood/Western Hills Goodwill, I had a Deaf coworker. I knew most of her interpreters from Finneytown High School or Cincinnati State College. **Most of my supervisors were learning sign language with my help to reduce dependence on the interpreters.** I hoped this coworker would be a good friend, and she was starting to become one until a manic episode got the best of her. That day, she was attempting to strike me and had to be held back by FOUR supervisors. I did not speak to her after this episode because I was worried that she may physically hurt me in the future.

At least 1 day a week at the Westwood/Western Hills Goodwill, I was in charge of all the cleaning of our break area at the back of the main room. I enjoyed that, especially when I simultaneously discovered new music thanks to our radio being on while I was cleaning. Another thing I enjoyed doing was working the Kutol machine, which assembles pumps for hand hygiene products because it was simple and the directions were clear.

Living Alone

My maternal grandmother was a good role model of independent living responsibilities because she lived alone in three apartments. She lived across town from us and I would go visit her. I was very close with her. I planned to keep my apartment a lot like she did.

I wanted to live in an apartment starting on my 18th birthday, but that wasn't realistic because my SSI hadn't started. My first apartment I ever rented alone was at Pine Terrace in the College Hill neighborhood of Cincinnati, Ohio. I lived at this apartment for 14 months, from March 2002 until May 2003. My SSI started on March 11, 2002, but the first rent of the month for the apartment was paid for by DD services. I left all the searching responsibilities for an apartment to my mother and service provider. The place was okay; the neighbors were really not nice and the police were there at least twice a week dealing with them.

I lived alone, which I loved, and I still love living alone. I enjoy living alone because it gives me complete control over my home environment, which I will insist on keeping for a LIFETIME. I NEVER want roommates or advanced technology taking that away from me! I remember being very happy and setting things up and arranging things how I liked it throughout my entire home instead of just in one room. I went shopping for furniture and other needs with my Mom, and I chose everything. **I felt very empowered to be able to make my own choices about my living situation.** I was at this apartment for 14 months and I liked it, but I really wanted to live in a vintage duplex because I like the older architecture. While I was at my first apartment I had some friends, who I met through the Cincinnati deaf events, visit my apartment.

One of my other apartments in Cincinnati was the largest one I ever had. It was half the first floor of a privately owned, two-story, two-family house. Cleaning for such a big place is overwhelming at times. Neighbor issues, especially nighttime noise, are often the most challenging for autistic adults, myself included.

Chapter Six

Life in Orange County, California

After I moved to Orange County, CA, before I met Sneha and began interning at Spectrum Success, a typical day for me began at 7 a.m. with breakfast and listening to Morning Edition from National Public Radio News. I first went to the Orange Public Library and History Center from 10:20 a.m.–12:20 p.m., returned home for lunch, then went to the Fullerton Public Library from 3:30–5 p.m. At the libraries, I spent most of my time on social media. I viewed photos posted by my favorite bloggers, like Becoming Minimalist, which often have printed words juxtaposed over an image. I call this type of photo a meme. I also read relationship advice blogs such as LifeHack.org. My favorite social network was Pinterest. In Orange County, I continue to live alone.

I reached out to Spectrum Success because I was tired of feeling like I cannot socialize outside Wellness Center Central, an adult mental health recovery day program in Orange, CA. I only attended the program on Mondays. I attended the gardening workshop and yoga class every Monday. Every other Monday, Vietnamese music was played from 12:30–1:20 p.m., and I listened to it unless I was talking to my friends. Every other Monday (but not the same Mondays as Vietnamese music is played), there was a smoking prevention class that is taught by the Wellness Center's Health Educator. He encouraged even nonsmokers to attend as most of the content is actually stress management and prevention techniques.

Attendees of the program are called members, and most of the Wellness Center members have bipolar disorder in some form and were born before 1970. That causes generational conflicts between me and them. **The lack of peers diagnosed with Asperger Syndrome makes most of the Wellness Center members almost impossible for me to relate to.** Outside of that program, every person I try to meet asks, "What do you do for <u>work</u>?" or, "Where do you <u>work</u>?" The only accurate answer was, "I don't work." I started feeling a stronger need than ever before to change that because the conversation died every time I revealed that I don't make money. **It made me feel like in Orange County, California, you ARE your job, and without one nobody wants to know you at all**, even if you qualify for and receive SSI and are not homeless.

In January 2016, I was determined to change my way of life for the better. I had just failed at having the first-ever serious relationship of my life. Knowing that another woman would not tolerate me using my diagnosis as an excuse for not working at all, I had to get something part time at the very least. So, upon reading Spectrum Success' website as it appeared at that time, I felt I would be understood best by Sneha and her start up. At that time, I reached out to Sneha to help me develop the employment skills I would need to seek employment. When we first met, I discovered that Spectrum Success was actually not a fully functioning program yet due to lack of funding, but I offered my experience and expertise to attempt to move Spectrum Success toward becoming a fully functioning program. I did this because I just wanted something else to do besides attending mental health programs. Sneha told me that she could learn a lot from me and valued my input toward the program. Due to lack of funding, we got creative, and in exchange for interning at Spectrum Success, Sneha coached me one-on-one in employment-related skills. I think everything that I learned from Sneha helped me in some way or another in my current job and employment.

When Spectrum Success offered me an internship in marketing, I was excited and smiling.

I started interning with Spectrum Success on January 28, 2016. Spectrum Success is an organization that helps autistic folks learn the skills to find jobs that they are interested in and teach them the tools to stay at those jobs long term. Spectrum Success also focuses on training employers and colleges to create more inclusive environments. I have even been a guest speaker during a class that Sneha was teaching at Chapman University, called Valuing Difference in American Society. **Helping an organization that does these things has allowed me to make a difference for the better in the autistic community.**

As part of my internship at Spectrum Success, Sneha provided me with one-on-one job coaching. Part of this included figuring out my strengths and interests to decide which type of career to pursue, and part of this included working on the skills that may help me obtain the job that I want. On April 6, 2016, I decided to see if attending "The Art of Active Networking" in Costa Mesa, CA would be a helpful networking experience for me. I found this event through meetup.com, which is a social network where offline gatherings are planned and publicized. You can connect with people who have similar interests as your own. I chose this one because the facilitator's description seemed to express understanding for those who dislike networking.

Sneha came with me to support me.

When I arrived, I was nervous enough, but was even more nervous when the facilitator said that we cannot sit next to someone we already know, or something to that effect. **Despite my auditory memory issues, if I imagine the printed images of the words I'm hearing, I can remember what was said, but I cannot always do that, especially if I'm tired or significantly distressed.** At this time I almost went into shutdown mode because of the many people, the simultaneous conversations (in particular, the volume of these conversations) made it impossible for me to gauge how well anyone was listening. Then, there was the added pressure of sitting next to someone that I did not know. **When I go into shutdown mode I become oblivious to the words and actions of everyone around me. All my thoughts become subconscious and I am not able to put them into words.** Even when I'm in shutdown mode I am able to look out for my safety, but I am not able to interact normally with anyone until I am out of shutdown mode.

Sneha noticed that this announcement made me uncomfortable, so we stepped outside to talk about it. She asked what I wanted to do, and I said that my first instinct was to leave but that I don't want to waste the $20 that we both paid to get into the event. Sneha explained that my reaction was a natural fight or flight response: to me, the situation was very stressful and my brain sensed that, and that's why my first instinct was to leave the stressful situation. She explained that there were at least three options that I could choose from, and that we would both do whichever option I chose: (1) Leave, (2) Follow the rules without accommodations, or (3) Use this as an opportunity to educate the facilitator about autism, and ask if it would be alright if I sat next to Sneha. I chose to ask the facilitator for an accommodation because the volume of all the simultaneous conversations was causing me sensory overload and I was literally about to go into shutdown mode multiple times. I didn't want to just leave because I had to pay $20 to attend this event and didn't want to be out that money. The facilitator was very accommodating and said he really cared about making me comfortable at his event. We truly appreciated how understanding and supportive he was. However, I was still uncomfortable with the volume of all the simultaneous conversations, which he could not reduce, so we left about halfway through the event.

At a professional development meeting with Sneha after the networking event, we reflected on the event. Sneha told me that she was extremely proud of me for pushing myself to attend these meetup events, and that she was impressed that I chose to stay and take the opportunity to educate someone about autism. When we were at the meetup and Sneha told me this, it made me feel better about staying. **I was able to stop myself from going into "shutdown mode" by reminding myself that I was there with someone I trust**. I do not enjoy making small talk, and this was what the networking event was all about. Sneha would ask me questions when we were talking in a group to get me to talk. This was difficult for me and she knew that. She was there to encourage me to practice the skills I need in the workplace. She acknowledged afterward that it was difficult for me, but that she was happy that I responded to her questions and again of how proud she was of me. She noticed that I did very well with making eye contact, and I told her that this was a skill that I have been working on for 16 years. Interacting with the Deaf community has helped me with my eye contact because the use of sign language requires it. I have been to more meetup events since this one.

Due to the stronger bias I perceive against sign language here in Orange County, I have given up my pursuit of a social life in the SoCal signing community because most of the sign language users I was meeting in the 2010s told me they resided in cities located in Los Angeles (LA) County. I do not feel safe on the streets or buses in most cities in LA County and do not plan to have a personal vehicle even once I am making money. I have since discovered the website of the Deaf Community of Riverside, which has convinced me that the SoCal signing community is actually in Riverside County, not Los Angeles County.

Employment

The only reason I believe I could not do a similar job as the grocery stocker at The Kroger Company nowadays is that I live in a border state full of families of three or more children under five who often run around in circles and squ**EEEEEE**al their little heads off in larger public spaces such as grocery stores. If I was being exposed to that all day every day, I'd have frequent headaches and be very stressed out. **I must clarify that any and all frequently occurring shrill noises give me headaches and stress me out. I need a job that keeps me away from overstimulation and high stress because of certain sounds**, if one exists. Most people with whom I discuss this issue just tell me to "face the truth that no such job exists." Sneha begs to differ, and so do I! Together, Sneha and I looked for job opportunities that would allow me to do my work without being exposed to certain noises, and we also worked on my coping skills when these loud noises stress me out.

My only sheltered workshop experience in Orange County was from 2010–2011 at My Day Counts (MDC) in Anaheim, California. The

Executive Director of the Alliance on Abilities' Integrity House pulled strings to get me into MDC so that I had an employer in the city limits of Anaheim to qualify for rental assistance. But due to the fact there was no work and mostly down time, MDC was unable to mark my paystubs with 40 hours a month of work, so Anaheim declined me for rental assistance.

At the time, I was exaggerating my auditory processing issues and refusing to communicate verbally at all, hoping I would be accommodated with sign language interpreters. I was still a lot more comfortable communicating through sign language than verbally. But there was a Deaf woman there for whom they refused to provide this type of accommodations, claiming they couldn't afford it. I realized that they would also refuse to accommodate me for similar reasons.

At MDC, my coworkers walked with abnormal gaits, causing their shoes to squeak quite loudly with every step. According to my then primary-care doctor, I literally developed stress- induced hypertension because I was only tolerating the shrill noises and subsequent headaches in hopes that I would get rental assistance.

On April 27, 2016, I participated in a group interview at The Salvation Army's Adult Rehabilitation Center in the eastern region of Anaheim, California. When my job developer at Westview Vocational Services informed me that I was to report there, she called it a job fair, not a group interview. So I did absolutely nothing to prepare for an interview, not knowing it was actually going to be an interview. She just texted me the day before, basically saying "There's a job fair at 1300 South Lewis Street in Anaheim, California tomorrow at 10 a.m. Come!" She gave no reassurance that it was optional, so I acted as if it was mandatory participation in my vocational program at Westview Vocational Services.

Myself included, there were approximately six participants. We were all asked if the current employment we stated on our applications was correct, which we all affirmed. We were all asked if we had transportation to the facility should we get hired, and we all said yes. We were all asked if our current employment would interfere with their availability to The Salvation Army. Since one of the main goals of my internship at Spectrum Success was to gain long-term employment that

I wanted, I clarified that my internship at Spectrum Success is one that I can telecommute from wherever there's internet, and it currently does not have specified hours during which I perform the duties. The interviewer stated that his current employees often strike up conversations over their work, slowing and even sometimes stopping production. We were all told that when the HR person returns from her approximately week-and-a-half vacation, we will all be called for second interviews.

Before the interview, I was calm, not nervous or anything. During the interview, I became nervous that I would not have a satisfactory answer when asked, "Why do you want to work here?" or "Why should we hire you?" But, surprisingly, those questions were never asked of any of us in the group interview. That was a relief for me.

After the interview, my job developer and I agreed it looked promising, especially because the interviewer expressed dissatisfaction with the performance of many of his current employees. I was proud of myself in how I answered the questions. I remained hopeful but not excessively optimistic that I would be called for a second interview. Once I left The Salvation Army's Adult Rehabilitation Center, I went to Starbucks to go online before attending groups at Wellness Center West in Garden Grove, California. It is another adult mental health recovery day program that works collaboratively with Wellness Center Central in Orange, California, which I mentioned in previously.

The job developer who helped me get the interview knew that I wanted to work a predominantly THINGS job, which IS the nature of warehouse work. At this time, I had FOUR job developers assist me in seeking employment: Sneha was both my supervisor AND one of my job developers, I had another one at Westview, and I had one at each of the Wellness Centers.

I would like to add that if you tell the California Department of Rehabilitation that you do not own any formalwear (interview appropriate clothes), they will write up a purchase order specifying a retailer that you go to and pick your own formalwear. I went to the retailer alone, but others have the option to be accompanied. The purchase order may send you to a chain store, but you must go to the location specified on the purchase order to use it as your form of payment. The purchase order will specify items you may purchase and quantities of each item.

The retailer will be unable to accept any returns whatsoever of items purchased with a purchase order, so be sure to try everything on and be sure you're comfortable with the fit of all items before having the cashier ring everything up and charge it to the purchase order.

During the second half of 2016 I worked at The Salvation Army. During 2017 I held several short-term jobs, mostly because they were temporary positions and I was only needed for a few days to a few weeks, which I knew going in. I found these jobs through various temporary agencies. Most of these jobs paid minimum wage. From December 2016–March 2017 I was completely out of work and back to my old way of life. Due to Sneha's complete bedrest during her pregnancy from January 2017–September 2017 I decided it was time to look for another job.

On job applications I stated my reason for leaving Spectrum Success as "not enough work." I was out of work completely until the end of March 2017, but I was still receiving Supplemental Security Income during this time. In March I approached a temp agency and was offered to work at Dahua Technology, a Chinese manufacturer of surveillance camera equipment intended for commercial use. I worked there for about a month, I was helping with a project and the project ended after a month. I was only out of work for about a week and a half before I started working at company D in May 2017.

The worst reaction I got from an employer to whom I disclosed my diagnosis was from company D. I discovered this job through indeed.com. I went for an interview that lasted about 40 minutes. They had two different positions that they offered me. One started at 4 a.m. and I told them that was too early. So I took the other position that started at 7 a.m. That position title was Wire Assistant. I'm not allowed to disclose what I did for this company. They told me this once I took the position, that I'm not allowed to even talk about what I do outside the department. I was only there for 3 weeks. I decided to disclose my disability because I could tell that D had a company culture of secrecy and I wanted to make sure they never put me in a position where I was expected to have more social interaction than I have the capacity for. I decided to disclose my disability 3 weeks into working there. I disclosed to my direct supervisor and HR via the in-house messaging system. A few hours later, I was let go. I asked why I was being let go and they told me it was nothing in particular, "it just wasn't working out." They never directly responded to my disclosure. I do not believe that me being let go was related to my disclosure because I was able to google some bad reviews of the company from other employees, one of whom had the audacity to bash the owner of the company by name in a public post. I think enough other people have had bad experiences working there that there may be some business circumstance that I was not informed of, which was the actual reason of me being let go. I was very upset when they let me go because they immediately stopped trusting me to go upstairs unaccompanied by HR to empty out my locker. I was ranting and raving loudly on the streets while waiting for a Lyft. I did not have the patience to wait for a bus that day.

After that I went 2 months afraid to work full-time again because I felt that I would need my SSI to fall back on. Then I got tired of not working, I had to have my cable and internet turned off because I could not pay the bill. I went back to a temporary agency, Randstad, and at first they wanted to send me to a place they had sent me before, but when that former employer did not accept me back, without stating why, they had to send me somewhere else.

Dahua Technology was the company that did not accept me back; I had worked there for a month during April 2017. So my next employer was Aminco. There was no interview because it was through an agency. I worked there for approximately a month assembling sports souvenirs. I enjoyed it somewhat even though I don't really care about sports at all. My coworkers were quite nosey about my dating life. I did tell them everything I felt comfortable telling them. They lied to me about their relationship statuses. I was the only male on the team. They later admitted that they lied. I don't think they were interested in me romantically because they had opposing religious and political views than me.

In 2017 I stopped working at my job at Aminco because I could no longer tolerate being the only male on the team after the biggest dating failure of my life. I had attended the first-ever event of a childfree meetup and one of the other attendees decided to complain about me,

I don't know who complained about me. I received a text the next morning from the organizer of the group stating that she had banned me from the group. I do not know why. She worded it, "I have to ask you to leave the group." This suggests someone else is obligating her to ban me, rather than her making the decision. I also feel that she was not taking responsibility for her action of banning me.

I became suicidal; this was September 9, 2017. I had gone there [the childfree meetup] to try to find someone to date. I responded to the text saying that "until I am told exactly what my offense was, I will not know because I have autism." The organizer responded that her brother also has autism, but I failed to consider that just because her brother has autism doesn't mean that she has a good relationship with him. At that time I had thought that if she has a sibling with my condition, she owes me a lot better understanding than she is giving. I responded and continued the conversation until she stopped responding. She refused to tell me who the complainant was but she said the complainant said I was rude, but she did not say how. Autistic demeanor is often mistaken as rudeness.

After this day I crashed and I burned. I was depressed for 2 months thereafter. I was having suicidal thoughts and 2 days later I checked myself into the ER. I was only there for 6 hours. They just increased my medication and sent me home. I felt a lot more tired with the increase in medication, but otherwise better. My suicidal thoughts did not continue but I was still depressed. I checked myself into the hospital because I was afraid that I would act on my suicidal thoughts.

I cried about all this on some childfree Facebook groups and got nothing but attacking responses calling me a stalker and a rapist. Some people even said that my father committed suicide, but that's not true, he's alive and well.

I got more jobs starting in October 2017 so I was only about 3 weeks out of work. I was running out of money and on top of that, social security misread my letters and believed that I was working at two places and was demanding $3,300 payback of a payment that I knew I did not owe. I went into the office and told them that I'm only working at one place; they had overestimated my income by at least three-fold. I did not have to pay them back.

I worked at various jobs over the next few months, but I was often more tired than my medications made me feel because I rarely slept well, having to stay up until midnight every night for one of these jobs. My hours there were 2–10:30 p.m. and it would take me an hour to get home via a combination of bus and biking. The whole experience was just too much. When I'm tired, I'm so irritable that doctors want to heavily medicate me and everyone is uncomfortable around me. People even accuse me of being "threatening" despite me NOT saying I want to harm them physically, and even assuring them that I do NOT want to harm anyone physically. So, I just have to isolate myself when I haven't slept well so that I don't alienate anyone. I did that job for just 2 months and then I quit. I emailed HR and told them I was resigning.

I was only out of work for about 6 weeks before starting at General Tool, where I currently work. I was applying with at least 10 different temp agencies in January of 2018 to find a job. I received a call back in the beginning of February 2018 from Talent Human Resources and they offered me my current position at General Tool. I went to the temp agency office because they required a drug test, I took and passed the drug test. I started working at General Tool the next day. I biked to the factory at 8:30 a.m. I woke up excited. I was told to meet with the Human Resources generalist, there was a short interview when I got there. I'm surprised my answers to the questions didn't cost me getting the job, because I wasn't even told that there would be an interview or that I had to fill out an application when I got there. I thought that I would just get there and start working. One question was "why so many changes in your job history?" And I said, "It's not my fault that the assignments I get through agencies are so short." The interview didn't last more than 15 minutes. They gave me the job immediately and I was happy to have another job. General Tool is a lot more competitive than the other jobs I worked; they try to keep you at least $1.50 above the current minimum wage. I feel that I am being compensated fairly there, and am even scheduled to receive a raise this year. I've never received a raise at any previous job.

At General Tool my first position title was Packaging Clerk. I packaged diamond tools, like circular saw blades, grinding wheels, polishing pads, and core drilling bits. Depending on the nature of the product and the customer's order, the product can be packaged in boxes or clamshells. I build the boxes because they come flat or in pieces. Larger blades are packaged between pads in a cardboard box. The pads get strapped first and then the box gets strapped. I'm also responsible for completing the shipping orders for one customer who always wants an itemized list printed on a label that is stuck to the outside of the package. Whenever the Lead Packager did not show up, I was also responsible for telling my coworkers which orders have been deemed urgent so that they get done on time.

I knew right away that I was going to loathe all my coworkers in the first department that I was assigned to, the production floor, because they are heavy slang users. Every sentence out of their mouths has to contain at least one f-bomb. **As an autistic adult I am very distracted by the constant f-bombs because I cannot figure out what they are actually trying to say.** On the first day I only spoke to the coworkers enough to understand what to do. **I discovered that my math skills would be useful in this department** because the diamond dust has to be measured to the decigram. I only worked on the production floor for the first 2.5 weeks because I was offered to transfer to packaging and I accepted the offer. I felt that I would have better coworker relationships in packaging because of all the cussing on the production floor. Also, it is quieter in packaging. **I have hypersensitive hearing and I don't tolerate noise very well. I knew right away I would get along a lot better with the packaging coworkers because there was a lot less cussing.** Everyone in packaging speaks Spanish and I speak Spanish so with everyone speaking Spanish in the packaging department, it was a lot easier to communicate. I learnt how to speak Spanish in middle school starting in sixth grade. I am fluent. Even though I could never get my classmates in high school to practice Spanish outside of class, I retained it.

While my coworkers in the packaging department are friendly, I still don't trust them enough to disclose a lot of personal things to them. One example is they have already asked me multiple times if I believe in God. I feel very awkward when asked and I tell them I refuse to discuss it or answer that question at all. They respond with silence for about a minute and then change the subject. There are about six people in the packaging department, but it can be up to nine if other departments are slow. In the production department there is usually a maximum of five people but on an average day, only four. In packaging we are usually working on our own, so we don't talk much. The more we talk, the more the upper management gets suspicious that we're not actually getting work done. I am enjoying the work itself, but I do eventually want to be driving a forklift, and hope to be able to do this at General Tool at some point. I have shown my fork lift certification to my boss, my shift lead, and one person above them. They remarked that my certification states some skills that are rare to them, such as knowing how to operate an electric pallet jack, which is a forklift not commonly used. It makes me feel good to be recognized for my special skill set.

On December 6, 2018, I sent the following email to my supervisors and the HR Manager at General Tool:

> Good Morning,
>
> This Sunday 12/9 marks 10 months altogether I have worked at General Tool. I remain thoroughly satisfied with my employment here. Back on my first day (2/9/2018) I did check the box on the application that says "Yes I have a disability." My disability is what is now called Level I Autism Spectrum Disorder. It obviously does not affect my performance of the duties of my Packaging Clerk position; however, you will notice sometimes that my social demeanor is very different from that of most others here.

This morning D. (temp stamper) called V. and put the call on speakerphone. I heard V. sounding very drunk. I informed J. and C. Then A., you exclaimed that I should know better? The abovementioned diagnosis is why I sometimes make moves like this. If it's really against company rules I won't do it again. I have read the Employee Handbook and saw what was said about malicious gossip. I hope no one is taking this as such as that certainly wasn't my intent.

The last time I told an employer in writing that I have this condition, they actually let me go. I often hesitate to reveal this to employers because of this experience plus my personal observation that there are many foul-mouthed people in this industry who fail to refrain from discussing their experiences with incarceration while on the clock. Ex-cons often treat me worse upon finding out that I have this condition. I just thought maybe disclosing may help you understand why I think social moves like the moment we had this morning are OK.

Adam Valerius

Packaging Clerk

Here's the positive response I got from HR. I thanked him for his reassurance complete *with* ☺ ☺ (Smiley faces)

Good Afternoon Adam,

We appreciate you having the courage to disclose your disability. You have nothing to worry about here. We appreciate the work you have done at our company, and look forward to continue working with you in the future. S will talk to you directly about what happened.

Please let us know if you need anything from us.

Disclosing my diagnosis was nerve-wracking at first due to my experience with D. But I just couldn't have my department lead saying, "You should know better!" every time I commit a faux pas. Newsflash: I have a valid medical excuse for my faux pas. I don't want to just snap at her like I would a stranger on the street.

I do feel deeply relieved like a weight is lifted and I am reciprocating the trust that my employer has given to me. I just didn't want to tell my department lead out loud, as then everyone would know.

The incident that led to my disclosure was when two other coworkers outside my department were asking me about a certain coworker inside my department. They were asking where he was because he had missed many days. I knew that he had been drinking heavily because a coworker in a neighboring department reached him and I overheard his slurred speech. I told the coworkers who were asking that he was sick. While I was speaking to the coworkers from the other department, my department lead was wagging her finger no in my direction, and I was not understanding what that meant. After the finger wagging, my department lead told me, "you should know better." **That is when I decided to send the email to HR because I did not understand why this was wrong, I saw no harm in it. So, that same day, I sent the email.**

I felt like it was because of my autism that I did not understand, there's no other possible reason. HR responded to my email that day. I sent the email to HR, my manager, my shift lead, and my department lead.

Nothing has changed for me at work because of my disclosure. Nobody really asks me about autism. **In the past when I have told other people that I have autism, they just go into denial because I work 40 hours a week.**

My current position as of 2021 is lead packager at General Tool, and I have held this position since July 10, 2019. I have worked there for about 3.5 years. It is the longest job I've had. It's the first job that's ever given me a performance review because I never kept all my other jobs long enough. My current way of life costs a lot more money than SSI will ever afford. And I just could not bear to give up. I was motivated not just by this but also **I always wanted to get as far as I could in the workforce. And I see my parents were both supervisors where they worked, so I never thought I would really get that far, but I have and I am proud of it.** Last year on my birthday, for the first time ever, my desk was all decorated with balloons and streamers and a happy birthday sign. I felt loved.

I think I get treated the same as everyone else at General Tool. I only notice any different treatment when I state certain boundaries that I have. Such as coworkers at my job calling me "bro." I respond, "I ain't your bro" because use of such a term suggests much greater closeness than coworkers or even friendship, neither of which I'd ever want with people who can't even utter one sentence without an f-bomb.

I feel like people at my current job can depend on me. **They frequently turn to me to unlock the supplies room because I'm one of few who's been trusted with the code.** And others who know the code are often too busy. **I do have a couple of coworkers who regularly ask me for help.** They just ask me where certain labels and inserts for packaging are located, especially when we begin to use new materials that we haven't used before. I think I have a good handle on things, they especially turn to me when they have trouble reading the English on the order papers.

The first time I wet the bed as an adult was back in January of 2019. I don't remember what I was stressed about, but it was something to do with work. The second time was Tuesday night, March 5, 2019, because I was stressed about the technology that I overheard my coworkers talking about, and I was doing both my job and my coworkers' job. I had been off my medication for a month and I was doing fine before this incident. On Friday morning, March 1, 2019, I overheard my supervisor quoting Elon Musk as having said, "Everything's recorded, so you can't deny you said something because there is a recording somewhere of you saying what you're denying having said," and "You will need to have a chip implanted in your brain to make sure you are controlling the machine and the machine is not controlling you." My supervisor remarked that if the latter statement ever becomes reality, he would be out of a job. Hey . . . I'd be out of a job quicker than he would, and for a lot longer, with my long history of using medical excuses not to work at all. That night I went home, googled these Elon Musk quotes, and discovered they were transcribed from the audio of a documentary titled, "Do You Trust This Computer?" which had been released about 11 months prior on April 5, 2018.

I took everything they said about the Elon Musk documentary literally; **autistic people are known to take things literally, I could not help it as I never can. I just could not get it off my mind.** I did not feel like I was going to have a heart attack. But I did feel like there was a possibility of my blood pressure causing a stroke within that day. I certainly vented out loud once I got out on the street during my break, and then later that evening I went to CVS and picked up my medication and started taking it again. I got rid of my iPhone and I put my MacBook away in the closet, one of the closets in my home that I rarely touch. I left it there for maybe a month. I don't remember how long. I started using technology again in July of that year.

I sent my Mom a message about this and fortunately she did not lecture me or talk down to me about my choice to stop taking the medicine, that she had almost always done in the past. I hate being back on the medicine, but I acknowledge my need for it at this time. It's more sedation than I need, even at the lowest available dose. I will continue to work with my psychiatrist to talk about a possible medication change so that I can take something that's not going to just knock me out at night.

Friendships and Romantic Relationships

In the Autism/Asperger's community, I may be in a minority when I reveal my cravings for physical affection. I need a new friend, preferably friend<u>s</u> plural, who give me 20-second hugs, which are said to be more beneficial than shorter hugs. I need to always have at least one friend who gives me 20-second hugs, whether I have a romantic partner or not. Due to societal norms about intimacy, this friend would ideally be female.

I used a service called the Snuggle Buddies in order to receive platonic touch, which increases my level of oxytocin. The Snuggle Buddies describe themselves as a platonic companionship service. FAQ #10 is, "Do we have to just cuddle?" and the answer is NO, that you can do any platonic activity, whether it involves touching or not. **When I discovered this service, I was excited because I know my dating difficulties are likely to last a lifetime. I have been researching the NEED for touch for 11 years and counting.** An hour appointment with one of The Snuggle Buddies' professional snugglers would be enough time for us to mutually exchange foot massages and snuggle. During our snuggle we both remain fully clothed and do not kiss at all. Just three hour-long sessions per year would have been all I could have afforded with saved-up spare SSI, but **it will at least prevent my depression from causing suicidal ideation despite my dating difficulties.** Though I have the option to apply for a job as a professional cuddler, I'm afraid it would worsen my dating difficulties. While Snuggle Buddies went out of business in early 2021, other cuddling firms still exist, and they usually require you to have a valid driver's license and a dependable vehicle, neither of which I have nor do I plan to obtain. **I currently feel that educating others on the need for touch is my strongest passion.** However, after attending Cuddle Sanctuary's workshops on August 27, 2016 and September 24, 2016, and receiving an hour-long berating phone call from their founder on October 2, 2016, I know that any sort of comparable workshop, including one hosted under the Cuddle Party branding, is nothing but a lecture overemphasizing consent outside of a sexual context. In April of 2017, I received a threatening message from a man who hosts workshops based on Cuddle Sanctuary's workshops via meetup.com's messaging feature, in which he said, "Any nonconsensual touching at my events will result in a call to the police department!" The treatment in the Orange County, CA jails outlined in the 2017 American Civil Liberties Union (ACLU) report is extremely disproportionate to a merely unwanted, yet painless and noninjurious contact. However, I simply acknowledge the breadth of the California battery law and disassociate with anyone who threatens to accuse me of the crime when I have not injured them.

I currently attend different Wellness Center groups and have friends there. H was the facilitator of one of the NAMI groups; she and I dated from August 2 till August 7, 2015. I decided to go back to the group in January 2019 because I had a rough week at work and didn't have any money to pay a therapist, so I thought I would vent in the group about my rough week at work. On March 9, 2019, she texted me out of the blue and told me she wanted nothing to do with me, I don't know why.

In 2010 I read **HappilyChildFree.com** *and discovered that I did not have to desire fatherhood just to have a romantic relationship. Upon telling a sign language student I was reading this in July of 2011, she asked me to have sex with her and told me her female classmates were telling her to ask me to have sex with her. I refused to have sex with her because* (1) the nearest place to my home that sells condoms had already closed for the night, (2) I did not believe her birth control implant was inserted correctly because it was bulging the skin of her arm too visibly and (3) I was presumably fertile and knew that half my SSI would be taken for child support had she become pregnant, carried the baby to term, and had me confirmed to be the father. At the time this would have forced me to be homeless or go move back in with my parents, which really isn't an option because they refuse to house me now that they are no longer legally obligated to do so.

So, I got a vasectomy because most people just make babies not considering if they are fit to be parents or not. I don't wanna be like that. **I know I will NEVER be fit to be a father because I just run away from a squealing toddler no matter whose it is.** If it's my squealing toddler I would go to prison for child neglect. Plus, I look back on all the times I woke my parents when I was 17 and could NEVER have a child, pet, or anyone/anything waking me. I don't return to restful sleep after being woke in the night like I assume my parents do.

I had researched the psychological impact of vasectomy. Wikipedia says it can increase a man's sexual desire. Prior to becoming sterile I had no desire to penetrate a woman. But within hours of waking up from general anesthesia on the day of my vasectomy, I was fantasizing about losing my virginity. I had developed the desire I denied having all those years. So once I was confirmed sterile on March 7, 2013 I began actively seeking to lose my virginity. On social media I was falsely accused by strangers of "being sexually entitled," "making untoward sexual advances," and even "objectifying women."

My first sexual relationship happened during the final third of 2015. I lost my virginity at the age of 31 on September 26, 2015 at 22:13 Pacific Daylight Time inside my home. My virginity taker admitted to having sexual fantasies about me since about 3 weeks after we met.

Fortunately, we took about 4.5 months to get to know each other before I boned her.

I felt relieved that I lost my virginity. I no longer felt desperate about getting to ejaculate inside a woman without impregnating her or demanding she take hormones that make her moody. When this relationship ended I felt that it was accurate to admit being completely inexperienced in serious and/or sexual relationships, so I still took 80 % responsibility for the failure of the relationship, only deflecting 20 % back to her when she blamed me 100 % for the failure of "us."

There's no map showing existence of a road called Breakup Boulevard, but in my imagination there is Breakup Boulevard North and Breakup Boulevard South. When a relationship ends, me and my partner are traveling westbound on Romance Road (again nonexistent outside my imagination) and are about to hit a guardrail straight ahead. One of us, who will feel more relieved about the breakup, turns right onto the onramp to Breakup Boulevard North, reaching up and pushing a garage remote button to make a gate slam behind their car. Then the other one is forced to turn left onto the onramp to Breakup Boulevard South to avoid hitting the guardrail.

When I ordered the breakup with my virginity taker on December 28, 2015, I was the one turning right on Breakup Boulevard North onramp and making the gate slam behind me. What vehicle was I driving in this imaginary thought process? A 1994 Geo Prizm LSi I had actually driven years 11 years prior in real life, still with Ohio license plate.

I have always compartmentalized physical touch away from sexual touch. You're not sexually touching someone unless touching the sexual organ, anus, groin, or buttocks of any person, and the breast of a female. Even California Penal Code 243.4 (g) (1) agrees with my compartmentalization. All other areas of the body are nonsexual.

The longest romantic relationship I ever had was with my virginity taker for 109 days from September 11, 2015– December 28, 2015. Going out shopping, going out to eat, engaging in public displays of affection, most conspicuously at Dave and Buster's on my 32nd birthday, made it the time of my life.

The first time me and my virginity taker broke up, I felt relieved but desperate for more cuddles and to have a woman enjoy my foot massage skills. Knowing I wouldn't have the money to hire a professional cuddler until July of 2016, I tried to just distract myself. At first it was difficult to distract myself because I tend to notice restaurant jukeboxes more than most people do. During one of my first meetings with Sneha at Starbucks' Hutton Centre location in Santa Ana, CA during February of 2016, they played Parson James' song, "Waiting Game." I do like piano ballads, but the lyrics really hit home for me, and 2 months later I had to stop listening to the song until after my first-ever session with a professional cuddler on July 16, 2016.

I didn't make a very clean break from my virginity taker when I ordered the breakup. So, 2 years later, on December 9, 2017 we got back together for a month, and it went worse than expected. Not only did we make love two more times, bringing my memorized count of acts of missionary intercourse to four rather than two, we had plenty of arguments in which she accused me of reveling in fighting with her. I knew I was making a mistake in obliging when she asked me to take my clothes off on December 16, 2017. I found myself f***ing [having sex with] her again. Our foreplay during act four, which occurred on December 22nd, 2017, involved me making myself extremely uncomfortable trying to get her properly aroused. She ordered the second breakup on January 16, 2018.

Relationship With Parents

The last major shouting match with my mom was approximately 10 years ago. It has been better now, although the worst conversation I ever had in my whole life that breaks all records was just a few years ago. That conversation was about my resentments of California Penal Code 242 (Battery) being overbroad. **I resented society as a whole.** Telling my mother was a big mistake on my part because she just started talking down to me and claiming I've been angry my whole life. When she made this claim, I took that as from the minute I wake up to the minute I fall asleep every day that I have existed, my emotional state has been nothing but anger, and that is not accurate. I did not tell her my thoughts because I figured she would not listen. But because of this conversation, for several years thereafter, she was the first person I thought of when I listen to Simply Red's cover of, "If You Don't Know Me by Now."

I think my relationship with my father has improved because he's getting old and he doesn't really want to think about the past. I no longer resent him for all those petty spankings growing up. I talk to my parents now at least once a month, but the conversations are about half an hour or less because there hasn't been as much family news since my maternal grandmother has been dead since September 29, 2016.

I look up to my maternal grandmother for teaching us how unconditional love is supposed to feel. Even when I demanded my parents give up on their relationships with me when I was 16 and 17, they never did. As my grandparents were dying, I decided to reassess and see if my relationships with my parents were still that bad and I concluded they're not. We still don't agree on religion, politics, or my personal history, but my parents no longer challenge everything I say as they did during my early adulthood. Specialists on whom my parents were relying from 1986–2005 were giving the worst possible advice any specialist ever could have given. But my parents have since deviated from that advice, allowing their relationships with me to improve as much as they have.

Concluding Thoughts

I think that the most misunderstood thing about autism is how it causes us to have this different social demeanor that is often taken as creepy. It doesn't seem to matter how we explain it, they're just gonna keep taking it as creepy no matter what. It's almost like they're closed minded. It's really not creepy because it is caused by a medical condition that is not curable.

And there are no pills we can pop for it either. One thing I want to tell the world about autism is that it manifests differently in each person that has it.

Growing up, I felt different because I felt I had reduced need for social contact. I was happiest just listening to recorded music and simultaneously admiring the vegetation. During the warmer months of the year I would do this in the backyard of the house where I grew up.

During the cooler months of the year I would just stare at the trees out the window of my room. I didn't feel that I needed friends.

I only wrote regularly until I started feeling ignored online after I finished interning with Sneha at the start of 2017. When I typed out my frustrations on the night of December 11, 2001, I was only typing a Microsoft Word document on my Windows laptop I had at the time without an internet connection. I did so because I feared that my roommates and the group home operators would misunderstand my verbal stimming as a psychotic episode. **At the time I would verbally stim for hours at a time and anyone who heard would suspect I was hearing voices, even my parents at times. I have never heard voices that weren't there.** Verbal stimming is a way of organizing my thoughts in some way of regulating my emotions and keeping my thoughts organized. I try not to do it in public places because people misunderstand. According to my mother I have been doing it my whole life since my first words.

I still feel misunderstood today. I wonder if I will ever feel understood by most of the people in my life. I've just learned to cherish my relationships with people that actually strive to understand me. For the most part I do feel understood by some people, and I feel that Sneha is one of the few.

Part Three

What Does This Mean?

Chapter Seven

A Thematic Analysis of Adam's Story and Autobiographical Accounts

Chapter Two outlined my process of using grounded theory for in-depth analysis, and what each step of coding entailed. This chapter will focus on the in-depth analysis of axial coding of Adam's autobiography and the constant comparison method of the 20 autobiographies. The results of axial coding, combined with the autobiographical constant comparison model, led to the following categories and subcategories:

A. Isolation
    a. Mental Health
    b. Societal Expectations
    c. Medical Treatment and Diagnosis
B. Influence of Parents
C. Differences in Needs: Examples from Education and Employment
D. Empowerment
    a. Understanding One's Own Behavior Through ASD Diagnosis
        i. Sensory Experiences
E. Relationships
    a. Friendships

b. Romantic Relationships
  c. Parenting

Though axial coding of Adam's story led to two main categories, Isolation and Empowerment (with several subcategories in each), the same subcategories did not fit neatly into either main category when combined with examples from the autobiographical accounts. For example, although parental influence led to feelings of isolation for Adam and for some of the authors, authors noted their parental influence led to empowerment. Each of the categories previously listed is explored in detail in this chapter. To discuss the authors' experiences using these categorical contexts, it was first necessary to define the components making up each category. Each category has the following components defined and exemplified: (a) *contexts*— settings and boundaries where action and process occur; (b) *conditions*—routines and situations that do or do not occur in the contexts; (c) *interactions*—specific types, qualities, and strategies of exchange between people in these contexts and conditions; (d) *consequence*—outcomes and results of these contexts, conditions, and interactions. Defining components of each category serves to help readers understand if, when, how, and why something happens (Saldaña, 2016).

Just as important as defining these components was detailing experiences that exemplified each category. After each category was defined, I provided several examples provided from Adam's story and the 20 autobiographies to help readers understand the lived experiences of autistic people. Defining the components of each category was not meant to be a comprehensive understanding of relevant experiences, but rather, to guide readers through the autistic authors' experiences and reflect major patterns in these experiences. According to Glaser and Strauss (1967), "categories should not be so abstract as to lose their sensitizing aspect, but yet must be abstract enough to make (the emerging) theory a general guide to multi-conditional, ever-changing daily situations" (p. 242). The detailed accounts described in each section, understood using contexts from each category, led to the final step of grounded theory analysis: theory formation. These theories are explored in Chapter Eight.

Isolation

In Adam's stories and the autobiographies, experiences of Isolation were largely explained by the following four components:

- *Contexts*—The settings in which isolation most often occurred were psychiatric hospitals, institutions, schools, homes, places of employment, and sometimes within a marriage or friendship.
- *Conditions*—Situations often leading to isolation were rejection from peers or romantic partners, being victims of bullying, lack of explanations for social rejection, forced to abide by societal expectations, exclusion from treatment planning, and misdiagnoses.
- *Interactions*—These included exchanges between autistic people and service providers, medical personnel, teachers, parents, friends, and partners. The exchanges were usually one sided, in that the autistic person did not have much of a say in how an event played out or they were rejected without being told why. Specific examples of experiencing isolation are explored in the remainder of this section.
- *Consequence*—As a result of contexts, conditions, and interactions, many authors, including Adam, experienced mental health issues such as depression and anxiety, feelings of shame at not being able to fit in, feeling misunderstood by society, resentment toward parents or peers, and feeling like they lived in their own world because their differences were not accepted by society. Mental Health, Societal Expectations, and Medical Treatment and Diagnosis are listed as subcategories for Isolation because they were consistently intertwined with experiences of Isolation.

Kanner (1943) first described autistic children as having "shown their extreme aloneness from the very beginning of life, not responding to anything that comes to them from the outside world" (p. 248). Because of this seminal assertion, stereotypes autistic people prefer solitary activities have persisted; these stereotypes, however, do not account for differences between engaging in activities alone versus loneliness. For example, Kim (2015) explained,

> Yet, when I'm alone, I rarely feel lonely. If I were writing the thesaurus entries for alone, the synonyms would include: authentic, free, individual, indulgent, open, peaceful, protected, pure, quiet, rejuvenating, solitary I observe and absorb the world around me. I'm good at being alone. The sense of inner security this creates is one of the hidden gifts of Asperger's. (p. 56)

Adam described instances of preferring to engage in activities on his own, during both childhood and employment, but he also described often feeling isolated, misunderstood, and craving connection and intimacy in the form of a relationship. Several authors described similar feelings—namely, how being misunderstood by society led to feelings of isolation and loneliness (James, 2017; Kim, 2015; Lawson, 1998; McKean, 1994; Mukhopadhyay, 2000; Prince-Hughes, 2004; Schneider, 1999; Shore, 2003; Willey, 1999; Williams, 1992).

Adam's feelings of loneliness were apparent throughout his story, and this isolation has continually impacted his mental health. Adam described his adolescent experiences of hospitalization in the psychiatric ward for behavioral outbursts, which eventually led to institutionalization at age 16. Both at those hospitals and at Buckeye Ranch, Adam felt isolated, lacked sense of belonging, and also reiterated they did not benefit him. He compared his experience living at Buckeye Ranch to living in a jail cell. He also recalled the psychiatric nurses using physical force with him. Adam's placement in these settings despite his resistance contributed to his verbalized loneliness, feelings of being misunderstood, and growing sense of resentment toward his parents.

Adam struggled during college, where he earned a certificate in deaf studies, because his peers were far older than he was. He felt there was a generational conflict, but also, in hindsight, believed certain psychotic medications he was taking caused him to have outbursts during classes. When he was informed that he often distracted his peers in class, Adam tried to explain his Asperger's diagnosis and how it affected his behavior. Yet again, he did not feel his explanation was heard. Instead, he felt misunderstood by his peers, teachers, and school administrators. He also continued to feel misunderstood by his parents, recalling an incident that led to him moving out of his parents' home and into a group home. This experience angered him and left him feeling as though he was not loved.

Several authors described feeling as though they lived in their own worlds, and their worlds were different from the neurotypical world; others described feeling like an alien from a different planet and how these differences led to feelings of isolation. One such example arose when Blackman (1999) said, "The realities of life reasserted themselves. My sensory and reasoning differences still left me moving as an alien in the human urban environment" (p. 123). Craft (2018), like Adam, mentioned despite occasionally being surrounded by people, she still felt isolated:

> I grew lonelier. Though there were people nearby, I nonetheless remained isolated in thought. It seemed that no one understood me The later years were painfully difficult.
>
> When the teenage trials came, I felt bombarded and stampeded with emotions. If there was ever a time I believed I was from another universe, it was then. I played a game- that is how I saw it. I pretended to be someone. I was lost, lost on some stage, trying to find where I'd hidden my true self. I still feel as if a part of me is hiding somewhere, afraid to come out entirely for fear of misunderstanding and judgment. The tender part, the piece that doesn't understand in the smallest degree the cruelty and harshness of this world – she remains divided and alone, hidden behind the curtain. (p. 44)

Lawson (1998) articulated how lack of understanding between two worlds led to isolation and depression. She desired connection and understanding, but when she struggled to achieve these feelings, she withdrew further into her own world, noting,

> For most of my life I have lived with a sense of being different and distant from my family and those around me. To my family, I was always different because I lived in a world of my own and seemed unable to relate socially as other children did. My sense of isolation and depression grew with time. I went deeper into my own world for some sense of reconciliation and self-comfort. (Lawson, 1998, p. 12)

In her book, Williams (1992) often wrote about loneliness she experienced. For instance, she discussed how her different means of processing events led to feeling like she was from a different world:

So little of what had happened around me had actually reached me. Even when anything happened to my body, it was as though my body was either a mere object existing in "the world" or, at other times, it was a wall between "my world" within and "the world" outside. (Williams, 1992, p. 94)

Dumortier (2002), whose book title included the phrase, *From Another Planet,* pointed out feeling accepted is a privilege many people take for granted. Lack of societal understanding of people with different social norms catalyzed feelings of ostracization. As she described:

I don't understand the world and the world doesn't understand me. I'm angry at the world and the world is angry with me. I'm not allowed to be a part of the world, but I still fight for the privilege, even though I know I will never win. I'm different and there's no room for me. The harder I try, the more frustrated I get. I will always be separate from the rest.

I will remain separate from that big, unattainable world. I will stay on my own planet. (Dumortier, 2002, p. 97)

Similarly, Prince-Hughes (2004) pointed out ostracization people face when they are perceived as different:

Maybe it is because so many people share the same past and dream the same dreams that they forget how lonely it can be to have a different past, a different dream. I knew what it was like to be in a prison. I knew because I was looking at it now with one foot outside the door, knowing the other would always remain inside. (p. 96)

McKean (1994) even wrote a song reflective of his yearning to connect with peers. The lyrics included:

I want so much to be a part of your world. I want so much to break through. And all I need is to have a bridge, a bridge built from me to you. And I will be together with you forever, and nothing can keep us apart. If you build me a bridge, a tiny, little bridge from my soul, down deep into your heart. (p. 37)

Other authors also expressed their loneliness via art. In a poem, Mukhopadhyay (2000) expressed how he was shunned from society for having different ways of processing the world. The poem read, "All the world was a busy place, and I was an idle kind, disqualified in the human race, a different form of mind" (Mukhopadhyay, 2000, p. 65).

Some authors described trying hard to fit into neurotypical societal norms and hiding their true selves. Yet, inability to fully conform led to feelings of shame and failure, as Dumortier (2002) noted:

> I would love to behave like most other people, but I find it impossible . . . the natural order of society doesn't make sense to me at all all my life I have been fully aware of the fact that I am outside the world, in other words, I am not part of it I try to conform and behave in the way any other person would I cannot be who I want to be;
>
> I have always hidden my true nature. I was always given the blame and therefore I believed it was me who was wrong. Sometimes I was ashamed of myself and I wanted to hide because I felt worthless. I was always on guard, thinking nobody wanted me. (p. 11)

Hale (2017) thought she would be able to fit in better with her peers when she went to college, but remained just as misunderstood, noting,

> I am lost within the frustration at my failure to cope with university life. I thought if I escaped to university, life would be much better, away from the hassles of home, but I have discovered that I cannot escape from myself. Now I have time to reflect. Why me? What did I do to deserve this affliction? Will I ever find a niche in life? Will I ever be able to effectively communicate in words? I wish that I could communicate. I wish someone could understand me. What can I do to become a 'real' person who is able to interact and join in life's rich tapestry of activities? (p. 99)

As with Dumortier (2002) and Hale (2017), Prince-Hughes (2004) felt shame for not fitting in, which drove her to even stronger feelings of isolation:

> My parents tried to come to check on me as best they could and bring me things to make my life easier, but I was losing contact with them, moving away from them and into nothingness. I was ashamed that I couldn't function, and sometimes I avoided them when I knew they were coming This was the beginning of several lost years during which I was homeless. I traveled all over the country, staying with people who took pity on me or saw something in me. (p. 65)

James (2017) highlighted what a toll it takes on autistic people to constantly try to meet societal expectations:

"I feel physically worse than I have for years and emotionally so less regulated than usual. I am tired to my core. I'm sad and I'm sick of my body and my brain. I just want everything to stop." . . . I can't go on like this. I am burnt-out and exhausted. This, I have read, is common in autistic people, particularly those who have struggled for years to "pass." It is called the cost of passing. It is essentially exhaustion brought on by the extra strain of pretending to be something one is not. (p. 189)

James also recognized her routines helped her navigate the world, but also made her feel trapped: I am a prisoner to my routines. Why can't I be like normal people and go to the coffee shop at different times? . . . The fact is, if I don't go to the coffee shop at 8 a.m., 11 a.m., and 4:50 p.m., my day is ruined. It is having a map for the day that makes me feel safe.

But it's also a prison I have built for myself. Within its walls, I feel claustrophobic and sad. (James, 2017, p. 90)

When speaking about her experiences in junior high, Grandin said, "Perhaps because this time in my life was most unhappy, I recall only fragments A sense of isolation envelopes me" (Grandin & Scariano, 1986, p. 55). Though she was not able to retain specifics of her experiences, penetrating feelings of isolation stuck with her over time. Dumortier (2002) also felt her differences led to isolation, which was a scary and painful realization. She noted:

I'm imprisoned in my head and will stay there. I will never escape. I want to get rid of my head. . . . I don't understand the world. Everything scares me; the things I have to do on my own fill me with dread. Nobody ever really comes close to me. I will always be different. Inside I will always feel different. I am alone, quite alone, and that hurts. The wall cannot come down. It stays there. Forever. (Dumortier, 2002, p. 95)

In Grandin's case, it was evident she was penalized for her differences when the school principal called and expelled her. She recalled, "Mr. Harlow hadn't even asked to hear my side of it. He just assumed that since I was 'different' I was entirely to blame" (Grandin & Scariano, 1986, p. 60). Jackson (2002) described having body image issues, and this compounded isolation she felt related to her other differences:

> For the first time I was content in my body, even though I couldn't say the same about myself. The feeling of isolation, and the blatant flaws in my psychological structure, still tormented me, but at least I could look in the mirror and like what I saw in the physical sense. (p. 41)

Mental Health

When Adam first moved to Orange County, CA, he felt judged for not having a job. He felt people did not want to be friends with him when they learned he was unemployed. Later in adulthood he recalled how rejection from peers and potential romantic partners at times led to depression and suicidal ideation. When Adam recognized his suicidal thoughts, he felt afraid he might act on them but was able to seek support from a hospital. Eventually, stress from work and depression related to feelings of isolation led to two bedwetting episodes. Adam highlighted how misunderstood he has felt throughout his life and noted not understanding why he had been rejected by certain peer groups.

For many authors, including Adam, this sense of isolation and loneliness led to mental health issues such depression, anxiety, or suicidal ideations or attempts (Jackson, 2002; Lawson, 1998; Slavin, 2018). Mental-health-related issues have several different causes, and this section explores many instances of feeling isolated and subsequent mental health issues Adam experienced. Findings from Hossain et al. (2020) relatedly observed comorbidity of ASD and anxiety disorders, mood disorders, depressive disorders, and suicidal behavior (Hossain et al., 2020). Prince-Hughes (2004) explained how mental-health-related issues can arise from trying to conform to societal expectations, thereby suppressing one's true self:

> Like others who seek to be what they are not, we invariably end up with secondary problems engendered by chronic anxiety. As rage and frustration are pushed below our consciousness, we suffer depression. Somatic difficulties like stomachaches and headaches and other ailments can be chronic as a result of unrelenting anxiety and the repression of coping mechanisms while trying to fit in. Painful memories of past failures to be normal, and mounting evidence of our inadequacies, our failed attempts to "fit in," dog us. Comfort comes, oddly enough, in the form of increasing compulsions and a fierce rigidity that may cover the trail leading back to their causes. (p. 32)

In Prince-Hughes's case, she used alcohol to self-medicate, dropped out of high school, and ended up enduring homelessness for many years, which she said compounded her sense of loneliness to a degree she had never felt before. Like Adam, Birch (2003) had suicidal thoughts after struggling to develop relationships with peers:

> My mood was more often down than up. I felt desperate for friends and for other people, but I knew that I could not cope with people when I had them. This caused me to feel there was no solution to the loneliness I felt; and my failure at relationships of various kinds had caused my self-esteem to plummet. I arrived at the space where I did not want to live any more, and I had thoughts of ending my life. (p. 54)

Hale (2017) tried to use logical reasoning to plan an end to her life in case her circumstances did not improve by her 18th birthday, explaining:

> The time has come to enter the big wide world. Using a foundation of logic, I have plucked up enough courage to decide to wait exactly one year before reassessing the suicide issue. If it is true that my working life is much worse than my school life, I will end it all before my 18th Birthday. The logic in my mind has blocked out all fears, therefore I neither fear nor feel anything. (p. 70)

Jackson (2002) detailed ways in which she would self-harm to alleviate emotional pain.

Although she did not attempt suicide, her thoughts were indicative of suicidal ideation:

> I've already taken various methods of suicide into consideration. There's no outlet for the frustration I feel inside. I want to smash everything in the house. I want to slit my wrists. I want to put a bullet in my useless brain. I could number the reasons why. (p. 62)

Lawson (1998) described her friendships as all-consuming, but some friends were not able to cope with this style of friendship. When one friend stopped responding to her, Lawson became suicidal, admitting:

> At the age of 20 I attempted suicide, feeling no reason to continue with life. My source of life had gone. Maggie had decided I was strange and had demons inside me. She did not stay in contact and when our paths crossed at a later

date she would acknowledge my presence. Her behavior was too difficult for me to understand and her rejection of me too hard to cope with. (p. 75)

Slavin (2018), who suffered from clinical depression for much of his life, described his suicide attempt as not being able to cope with pain of life. His suicide attempt stemmed from wanting to correct his relationship with a previous girlfriend, because, frustratingly, he was not able to communicate clearly with her:

> And any words that did escape from my frozen mouth, did so, in a kind of confused, clumsy stutter. And for the second time in six-months, my pathetic social skills had destroyed any chance of ever being with her. It's not that I wanted to die, as such. It's just that I couldn't bare the pain of living any longer. I lay on Mick's bedroom floor with blood oozing from five gaping wrist wounds, and waited for the end. (p. 145)

Williams (1992) suffered from depression and also cut her wrists to alleviate emotional pain. She described her depression in the following passage:

> I fell into a deep depression which lasted about a year. I returned to my old school but hung about on the outside of any groups which tried to involve me. I stopped smiling and laughing, and the efforts to involve me only hurt me more, till I'd stand there with tears silently rolling down my face. At home I'd go up to my room and cry, saying over and over again. "I want to die." (p. 40)

For some authors, lack of access or understanding of specific needs led to panic attacks or other mental-health-related stress. For Grandin, this stress began manifesting itself in many different areas of her life and led to frequent panic attacks. She stated,

> The real world had become terrifying – out of control. Each day became more unpredictable. I longed for relief, but I was trapped by physical distress. Stress showed in my speech, my actions, my relationships with others. (Grandin & Scariano, 1986, p. 75)

Jackson (2002) had an entire section in her book on loneliness, which included the following excerpt from her diary:

> It's a feeling akin to severe loneliness (and I know loneliness plays a significant part in it) combined with deep-rooted self-hatred and a fear of stillness .

> . . I think it's not so much the silence as the loneliness that causes the problem. I feel so alone most of the time and the feeling is exacerbated late at night when my parents have gone to bed, it's too late to call my friend; there's no decent TV or movies to watch so I can't use the TV as substitute company; and there's absolutely nothing to occupy me except to go to bed and try to sleep. It's just a plain, blank, drowsy nothingness – a feeling so present that it's actually an all-pervading (and all-encompassing) entity in itself. Its very existence seems to dampen everything around me. Everything is dull and lifeless and still – and this concept kind of frightens me. (p. 57)

As outlined in the previous chapter, many authors dealt with bullying, which had profound impact on mental health and feelings of isolation. Prince-Hughes (2004) described one such bullying encounter:

> People would corner me in the bathroom and force my head into the toilet, slam me into my locker, and throw trash at me in the hall. They hit me in the head with books and spit on me. They defaced my locker. They took my food away. Once some senior students made a sign with a derogatory word on it and hung it around my neck. I didn't take it off. I walked around with it on because they had no power over me I was swimming in a sea of ugliness, hate, and intolerance – what good would it do to remove a cardboard sign? This kind of behavior never failed to confuse me. (pp. 60–61)

Jackson (2002) detailed several encounters with bullies, including:

> The manipulation process repeated itself at secondary school, but in different ways. . . .suddenly, a large group of my peers would burst out of the store cupboard, grab the food out of my hands and smear it on my face and in my hair, whilst spitting at me and pelting me with soggy chewing gum, and tipping sachets of pepper and salt over my head. Then they'd spring off, leaving me huddling under a table, sobbing, whimpering, rocking back and forth, too terrified to run to a teacher. The bullies would put ants, worms, maggots or even wasps in the drinks. (p. 25)

In an excerpt from a poem he wrote, McKean (1994) described the conundrum of not necessarily wanting to interact with people, but also not wanting to be alone:

> I know that you are lonely, and I know that your life is dull. I know that your past has given you fears and your back is tight against the wall. I can tell by

your looks you are hurting, I can see by your eyes that you're stoned. And it's hard when you don't want to be with people and you also don't want to be alone. Though it's hard to go on living when your life has been untrue, you can do it, Dreamchild, I have faith in you. (p. 94)

Willey (1999) also acknowledged she did not mind doing things on her own, but constant rejection from her peers was overwhelming. She did not understand why she could not make or keep friends, and to complicate matters, feelings of self-blame in response to not being able to make friends angered and confused her:

I saw I was invisible. On one level, this did not bother me. I liked my personal space. But, day in and day out, rejection began to lay heavy on my shoulders most likely because I did not understand why I was being excluded. To choose to be left out is one thing, but to be locked out, is quite another By the second semester, I began to feel too detached, too close to lonely. It made me very angry to learn this. (p. 56)

Willey's college experiences ultimately led to anxiety attacks, but she was able to find the right supports to help her socially, which in turn helped her academics. As she described:

My slow descent into total confusion and overwhelming anxiety attacks did lead me to a visit with a counselor on campus who gave me some of the best advice I ever received. She told me I needed to assess my strengths and weaknesses, to chart what I wanted to do and how I could do it, and to lay a plan for success that was reasonable and probable. (Willey, 1999, p. 64)

This chapter was labeled to align with the Isolation theme because Adam specifically mentioned "isolation" when describing many of his life experiences. Like Adam, several authors experienced loneliness, suicidal attempts or thoughts, and related mental health issues such as anxiety and depression (James, 2017; Kim, 2015; Lawson, 1998; McKean, 1994; Mukhopadhyay, 2000; Prince-Hughes, 2004; Schneider, 1999; Shore, 2003; Willey, 1999; Williams, 1992). Feeling misunderstood by society further compounds feelings of isolation. For some authors, not understanding why they struggled to connect with peers or communicate their experiences with loved ones also contributed to feeling misunderstood and as though they were living in their own worlds (Blackman, 1999; Craft, 2018; Lawson, 1998; Williams, 1992). Others felt ashamed they were not able to fit into the neurotypical world, and this also exacerbated their isolation and mental health issues (Dumortier, 2002; Hale, 2017; Prince-Hughes, 2004).

Regrettably, feelings of being misunderstood by society at large were reflected by most of the stories, including Adam's, and this rejection led to isolation and related mental health issues.

Societal Expectations

Throughout his story, Adam hinted at societal expectations and how they affected him. For example, he noted people have often been skeptical of his autism because he can work 40 hours per week. He also made a comment in Orange County, California, one is defined by their job, which was a contributing factor to his pursuit of employment. Prince-Hughes (2004) had similar experiences, stating,

> Because high-functioning autistic people may be invisible in this way, old stereotypes are reinforced, putting these people in an impossible position: if you can learn to interact socially, go to college, hold a job, and have a relationship, you can't possibly be autistic. Not only the public but even professionals who study autism are blind to the pain and cost, the silent desperation and continued psychological struggles that high-functioning autistics undergo every single day. (p. 31)
>
> James (2017) also had to fight the stereotypical view of autism as a barrier to success: Whenever I tell anyone about my autism the response is always the same. They are surprised. They can't quite believe it. I seem too much like them and too little like the stereotypical view of autism they know. They think I can't be autistic because I am married. Because I work with words. Because I have successfully raised my children. Or because I don't say anything offensive in conversation. I am not what they expect. I am not what I expect either and still, a year on from my diagnosis, I am fighting to live a neurotypical life. Where did it get me? Nowhere I wanted to be. I was sad, burnt-out, lonely, demoralized and confused. (p. 195)

Prince-Hughes (2004) described how many people rely on stereotypes about autism, despite how misguided these stereotypes are:

> Many people, again lay and professional alike, believe that all people with autism are by definition incapable of communicating, that they do not experience emotions, and that they cannot care about other people or the world around them. My experience, both personally and with others like me, is that in many cases quite the opposite is true. A significant number of autistic people who care deeply about all manner of things, and are profoundly emotional about them, share these capabilities in the privacy of their journals, diaries, and poetry. They do not show them to the world, which is too intense and often too destructive or, worse, dismissive. (p. 31)

Kim (2015) felt if she was judged through the lens of societal norms, she would not meet many stereotypes associated with autism:

> Decades passed and there I was, still waiting for someone to give me the secret handbook that would explain all those social nuances the people around me seemed to instinctively grasp . . . I'm happily married, a successful small business owner, and proud mom to a terrific young woman. Someone might look at those outward signs of success and wonder whether I'm really that autistic. Spend a day or even a few hours with me, and you'll stop wondering. (p. 14)

On August 18, 1988, Blackman (1999) wrote the following passage for her class assignment. In her prompt, she reflected on societal expectations related to normal behavior:
What's Normal:

> Will you feel that a person is normal if they show no initiative and if there is nothing special about them which makes them act differently from others or do you revel in the differences that make life interesting. I feel that the thing which makes us human is our differences from another. Perhaps though you belong to that group of people who would have us all be the same. Just remember that this is what Hitler tried to do. He was the cause of great suffering and the death of many because he did not like differences in people. Is this the world we want to live in? Surely our idea of normalcy should include a wide range of variations in all aspects of life. (Blackman, 1999, p. 129)

Slavin (2018) actually became obsessed with trying to understand the concept of normality, noting,

> My obsession with the concept of normality began in childhood, and more-or-less ends with the writing of this book . . . It turns out that normality is a relative state of being – largely defined by culture and belief. And that, at any time, new versions of normality can be forced onto a population, by those with the loudest voices, and the greatest power. But in the context of a discussion on autism, normality is largely judged on how we interact socially. Is our body language perceived as odd? And is our mode of communication consistent with what's considered typical? (p. 307)

On the topic of normalcy, Craft (2018) said,

> The idea of this concept called normal is one of the grandest illusions of our time. There is no normal. Normal doesn't exist. All definitions of normal are debatable – as are the definitions of typical, average, and ordinary. Normal apparently means behaving like most behave. But who are these most? And how do they behave? Show me the model. . . .Most mental health practitioners categorize and diagnose patients/clients by referring to the Bible of Abnormal – my word for the DSM. No surprise that the definition of normal changes with each publication of the DSM I am also a wee bit confused about the current definition of Asperger's Syndrome. The limiting definition is based on only male subjects. I'm a girl last time I checked. (p. 85)

Jackson (2002) used to get called a freak because of his differences, recalling,

> A lot of people who don't know that I have Asperger Syndrome say that I am a freak. Come to think of it, a lot of people who do know that I have AS call me a freak! Well aren't those open to interpretation?! What on earth is normal, usual or regular anyway? This of course comes back to the majority ruling, I reckon. (p. 35)

Dumortier (2002) reflected on how trying to abide by societal expectations of normal has impacted her daily life:

> Living in society is the difficulty. I try my very best to carve myself a place in this society and to learn some of its rules. But it's like installing a computer programme written in a different computer language. It's not compatible and you cannot make it compatible I am only seen as abnormal when I socialise with other people. Why?

Because I don't conform to the conventional picture. A picture created by the majority and which the majority decides is normal. But what is normal? (p. 101)

Mukhopadhyay (2000) felt guilty for not being able to conform to societal expectations, noting, "The constant guilt of not being able to be a proper and normal human being, was there too, standing in his way to 'try' and be like others" (p. 40). Additionally, despite trying her best to fit into societal expectations of normalcy, Hale (2017) was constantly mocked for her differences:

> Each day I try to act as normal as possible. Every time I slip up there is someone waiting to tell me how unintelligent or abnormal I am. The continual mockery from all sectors (especially at home and school) motivates me to try ever harder to behave within the expectations and boundaries of conventional society. There are too many constraints and protocols. Apparently everything about me is wrong, I get hassled for the way I speak, look, walk, behave. How will I ever manage to bridge the gaps? It is mind-boggling. (p. 56)

Prince-Hughes (2004) also elaborated on the concept of normal as a societal construct:

> I am glad that I am so successful at appearing normal (whatever that is), but I also wish at times people knew how hard I work at it. So much goes on that other people can't see. . . When I am not drawn in by another person's choice of topic, I often start thinking of things that I am more interested in and don't hear anything they say. I continue to have "sense addictions." I startle and must fight rage when someone touches me unexpectedly, and I still have a very hard time with groups of people. (p. 2)

Hall (2001) provided an excellent suggestion to reverse societal responsibility, thereby creating a more inclusive environment for people of all differences:

> Normal people should try harder to understand AS people because AS people have difficulties with some things most people find easy. They have to work very hard to understand normal people and behave normally. I know this because of how hard I have had to work on thingsPeople should understand

that it can be tough having AS. Small things can still really upset me sometimes. (p. 98)

Lawson (1998) noted, though she understood societal expectations, trying to constantly fulfill societal norms can cause a great deal of stress:

> Although it is still easier to hear people when eye contact is avoided, I do attempt to look at them during conversation. I accept this is a social norm in Western culture. With people I know well and have come to trust, eye contact is not so uncomfortable, but they will never understand the battle I have gone through to be able to do this. (p. 12)

Schneider (1999) felt he was punished by society for being different, disclosing,

> I have always been different, but, until recently, have not known why. Being different, in this sense, also implies having values that are not those held by society at large, and having social penalties exacted by that society for doing that. (p. 107)

Willey (1999) called for social acceptance for herself and autistic peers:

> My deep, dark fear, the one that makes my bones scream, is that there are AS people in search of friendships who will never find any, no matter what they do, solely because of their AS. With those people on my mind, my heart breaks, for I know the reality that will wound them as they stumble forward, deeply lonely and ever more estranged from others. I hope that, as society continues to break the boundaries of normal, the boundaries so many cannot see and so many cannot find, this blight which robs good people of growth and happiness will ebb into a distant hollow, unseen and forgettable. And then, maybe then, the world really will welcome all people. (p. 80)

Shore (2003) even compared being autistic to cultural difference:

> People are finely attuned to the norms and behaviors of their own culture. Those who do not follow these norms, perhaps due to an inability to read them, are shunned on a conscious level at the public school age and on a more unconscious level as one goes on to college and the workplace. I can only recollect one incident of bullying at the college level, while more have occurred after graduation. In the workplace, I made friends with foreign

people. I believe they accepted me more easily than Caucasian Americans because any subtle idiosyncratic behaviors I may have displayed were either not perceived or were attributed to being part of my culture. In addition, since people from other countries have their own challenges with cultural assimilation, they may be more tolerant of others' difference. (p. 81)

Mukhopadhyay's (2000) story also reflected the toll societal expectations can have on a marriage. Mukhopadhyay felt guilty he caused his parents to fight, but his parents explained to him their fights were triggered from societal views posturing autism in a negative light.

Mukhopadhyay's family was in India, and in Indian culture, parents are largely judged by actions of their children. He explained:

> Then he felt may be the arguments that took place between his parents were the cause of his inability to speak . . . But they did not fight or blame each other. Instead, they told him that it was after his problems started, that they began to argue over his "complexities in behaviour," resulting from the guilt of not parenting him well. They told him that they felt socially distanced because of him. (Mukhopadhyay, 2000, p. 37)

Although Mukhopadhyay's excerpt reflected how societal cultural norms interpret behavior, Prince-Hughes (2004) presented an example reflective of societal norms from a certain time period: "In the self-centered and aloof culture of the 1980s, my social impairments and my emotional and physical distance made me appear 'cool'" (p. 67).

Jackson (2002) pointed out socially appropriate behavior depends on who decides what is classified as appropriate: "Poor or no eye contact is seen to be a problem with social interaction, though I would dispute that. It is only a problem for those who want to be looked at" (p. 23).

Adam and several of the authors constantly had to respond to societal expectations of normal behavior and also fight stereotypes of what autistic behavior should look like (Blackman, 1999; James, 2017; Kim, 2015; Prince-Hughes, 2004). Many authors felt exhausted by constantly trying to figure out societal expectations and masking how they felt most comfortable to conform to societal norms (Dumortier, 2002; Jackson, 2002). Others felt guilty about not fiting into society, no matter how hard they tried, or were shunned and punished because they behaved differently (Mukhopadhyay, 2000; Schneider, 1999). Ultimately, it should not be the sole responsibility of the autistic person to conform to preconceived notions of normal behavior; rather, there should be mutual responsibility from everyone to respect differences.

Medical Treatment and Diagnosis

Much to Adam's chagrin, he was misdiagnosed with Psychotic Disorder Not Otherwise Specified (NOS) in addition to his accurate Asperger Syndrome diagnosis. The misdiagnosis of psychotic disorder NOS frustrated Adam because he knew it did not represent his behavior. He felt his parents and doctors misunderstood his actions and refused to listen to him as he tried to articulate what was actually happening. Doctors also prescribed him medications to address psychotic symptoms, but because he did not actually have psychotic symptoms, these medicines complicated his experiences rather than alleviating them. When he read about Asperger Syndrome, however, he felt the description accurately represented his experiences. He began to understand his behaviors in light of his diagnosis. Adam also described his early experiences with hospitalization, despite not wanting to be admitted to a psychiatric hospital. Exclusion from critical medical decisions created resentment toward his parents and mistrust toward his doctors, and exacerbated his feelings of isolation.

Adam described a lack of autonomy while in the psychiatric hospital, noting nurses there decided what defined acceptable behavior. For example, Adam noted up until his hospitalization, he preferred to be a loner, but this choice was not acceptable in the confines of the psychiatric hospital. Similarly, Birch (2013) described not being able to "hold her own space" (p. 48) while at the psychiatric hospital, explaining medical personnel had more power over her actions than she did. Birch (2003) also described medical personnel using a "one size fits all" (p. 116) approach, which ended up pathologizing differences rather than accepting them. Rajarshi (2000) described the power hierarchy between patients and doctors as, "doctors have the power . . .

patients are helpless to the whims of doctors" (p. 24). This hierarchy presents situations in which patients are unable to have equal say in treatment planning and are not treated with the same level of respect as doctors.

Like Adam, several authors described feeling different while growing up, but many did not know why they were different until their ASD diagnosis (Dumortier, 2002; Hall, 2001; James, 2017; Kim, 2015; Lawson, 1998). Relatedly, some authors did not know why they were different growing up, and this lack of insight led to isolation and confusion. Lawson (1998), for instance, noted, "My parents' lack of explanation only reinforced my belief about myself and withdrawal into my own world appeared to be the only thing to do" (p. 32).

Several authors, including Lawson (1998), Schneider (1999), Slavin (2018), and Williams (1992) were misdiagnosed with schizophrenia. Similarly, Adam was misdiagnosed with Psychotic Disorder NOS. Woodbury-Smith et al. (2010) explained schizophrenia and psychotic disorders have historically been common misdiagnoses for ASD. This misdiagnosis can occur because some characteristics of ASD, such as flat affect, may overlap with characteristics of schizotypal disorders. Yet, misdiagnosis can have lasting consequences when incorrect medicine, such as psychotropic medication, is then used for an autistic person (Woodbury-Smith et al., 2010), as was the case with Adam.

Isolation is a complex category with many intertwined components and outcomes. On the topic of medical treatment alone, Adam's experiences and the autobiographical accounts described lack of autonomy in treatment decisions, a hierarchy among patients, doctors, or parents, and frequency of misdiagnosis. Further exacerbating experiences of isolation were societal norms by which the authors were expected to abide, many times without explanation.

The settings in which isolation occurred were many, and conditions of the isolation, which included being victims of bullying and rejection from peers, were often difficult to read and process. As a result of these interactions and conditions, many authors experienced mental-health-related issues and ostracization by society while feeling as though they lived in their own worlds.

Influence of Parents

In Adam's story and in many of the autobiographies, it became clear that parents had substantial influence over their child's experiences—some for better, some for worse. Like other authors, Adam's parents seemed to be well meaning, but taking advice from therapists rather than listening to Adam directly sometimes led to friction with Adam. The category of Influence of Parents was positive for some, and negative for others. This category comprised the following components:

- *Contexts*—Most interactions happened in the home, at hospitals or clinical settings, or in relation to school and academics.
- *Conditions*—Some parents punished their children for their differences, whereas other parents advocated for their needs. Some parents did not believe in disabilities, and other parents tried to learn everything they could about autism and related support needs.
- *Interactions*—Interactions causing the most stress included physical punishment of children or shouting matches, without explanation as to what the child was doing wrong or how they could behave differently. On the other hand, though some autistic people felt dismissed by society as a whole, they recognized their parents saw their full potential and believed in them, which helped them succeed.
- *Consequence*—As a result of influence of their parents, certain autistic authors felt dismissed and misunderstood. These feelings occasionally led to resentment toward their parents. Conversely, other authors felt validated and supported, and appreciated their parents' involvement and advocacy. Specific examples detailing the influence of parents are provided in the remainder of this section.

In much of Adam's story, he spoke about childhood resentments. Although his parents disagreed with his assessment of verbal abuse, he felt both of his parents verbally abused him, and his father physically abused him in the form of spankings. He described instances when he took what his parents (or others) said literally, which led to confusion, anger, and fights with his parents. As with the previous chapter, this chapter also reflects Adam did not feel heard by his parents or by medical professionals and therapists who were treating him. He believed his parents sometimes spoke about him behind his back to doctors, and this angered him, as his voice was not heard or believed. Ultimately, Adam had great desire for personal autonomy, which he was not able to achieve during childhood.

Although Adam resents much of his childhood, he realized his parents were doing the best they could with advice given to them by medical professionals as he reflected back and read my notes from other autobiographies. Given many parents similarly follow guidance of medical personnel, it is crucial to include voices and experiences of autistic people in their treatment plans to ensure positive experiences and maximize successful support. Though some experiences were similar to Adam's, many were different. In my selection of autobiographies, authors described a mix of positive and negative experiences with their parents, many of which impacted them and their treatment in impactful ways.

Similar to Adam, Dumortier (2002) felt her experiences were frequently dismissed; she noted, "As a child I often tried to explain what had happened and I would always get the same response: that I was being silly or that I was lying. Nobody would listen to me" (p. 12). Although many of Adam's childhood experiences with his parents suggested tension and lack of understanding from his parents, it was also likely his parents were following advice given to them by medical professionals. This advice, as with the understanding of autism, has evolved over time. In earlier autobiographies, for instance, several authors mentioned their parents were subjugated to refrigerator mothers. In the 1950s–1970s, Leo Kanner, who played a significant role in differentiating between schizophrenia and ASD, blamed mothers of autistic children for causing their autism because they were cold, disengaged, and "lacked maternal warmth" (Cook & Willmerdinger, 2015, p. 2).

Adam described his fights with his parents as very intense, and Jackson (2002) had similar experiences, saying, "When my parents and

I argue, our arguments could top the Richter scale! They accuse me of having a temper control problem, yet they're too negligent of their own temper control" (p. 91). Jackson recognized it might be difficult for others in her family to cope with her specific needs, but expressed frustration because she felt like she was being punished for something she had no control over:

> My relationships with people have always been volatile, especially ones with family members. I can appreciate how tough it is for them having to deal with me and I respect them for their persistence, but half the time it seems like they're trying to put me on a guilt trip and that I should be apologizing for having this condition (I don't know if this is actually true, but it's just the impression I get). That angers me, because sometimes I feel like I'm being unfairly punished, serving a sentence for a crime I didn't commit. (p. 90)

Adam also resents the punishments and spankings he received as a child, but recognized the punishment tactics were perhaps due to advice of medical professionals. Similarly, McKean (1994) remarked,

> I fail to see why there was a strong lack of emotional support as I was growing up. But that support was not there. Or perhaps it was, but I certainly do not remember it. I was yelled at and punished quite a bit for what I did (and for what I did not do). (p. 3)

Williams (1992) described bewilderment at why she was being punished, noting, "Slap. I had no idea what was expected of me The world seemed to be impatient, annoying, callous and unrelenting. I learned to respond to it as such, crying, squealing, ignoring and running away" (p. 12).

Many parents tried their best to support and advocate for any treatment options they thought would help their child. Whereas some authors were not able to see or understand what parents did for them behind the scenes, others were able to overtly see their parents' support. Blackman (1999) was not able to communicate verbally, but after auditory integration training, she learned how to communicate via a typing device. She recalled a time her mom read a paragraph she wrote and the subsequent conversation:

> Her voice flooded and fluttered, "After seeing you type that paragraph, with its clear introduction and ending, with the thread of understated humour running through, and having such fun in writing like that, I don't think we can go on like this. If you like, I'll apply for funding for integration into a High School." I felt quite strange, as if someone had pumped air into me and I was floating in the morning sunlight among the soft green new shoots far above the road. (p. 117)

Whereas other people in her life dismissed her, her mom saw potential in her daughter and did everything she could to support her success.

Mukhopadhyay's (2000) mom saw potential in her son and did not give up on him despite what doctors told her. He noted, "Mother said she would not accept the fact that there was no 'use' teaching the boy, and she was certain that with right motivation he would be able to write also" (Mukhopadhyay, 2000, p. 30). Mukhopadhyay and his parents lived in India, where both of his parents revolved their lives around their son's access to care. When they had to move to a different part of India to receive long-term support services that had helped their son immensely, his dad lived in a different town to continue supporting his family, and his mom took to his care as an obsession, as he recalled:

> The mother was relieved that soon her son would be able to do more desirable things, that she began to lead a Spartan life. She got up at 4 am, finished her bath and half her cooking and then prepared a "goal" for the day. By seven the boy was up. After breakfast, the task began. There was no chance for the boy to get lost in his thoughts. If the boy tried to look away she hit him hard. That went on for days together. It worked.
>
> The boy became more attentive to her speech, and could follow her commands better. His father was unable to bear the sight, but he had great trust in his wife. So he went to another room without comment. (p. 19)

Despite suffering from agoraphobia and her own mental health issues, Shore's (2003) mom always worked hard to acquire necessary interventions and services for him:

> Mother also spent a lot of time talking and playing with me. Even though I didn't appear to be aware of her, she continued her efforts believing that, somehow, what she did was beneficial to me. This seemed to work as I slowly admitted her into my world. (p. 25)

Other parents advocated for better treatment of their children and understanding by society, because they realized if they didn't fight for their children, nobody would. When Grandin was at camp in third grade, her camp counselors made her parents aware of an episode in which she was repeating words other students were saying; some words were sexual in nature (Grandin & Scariano, 1986). Subsequently, Grandin was sent home from this camp. In response, Grandin's mom wrote a letter to her daughter's child psychologist. Excerpts from that letter reflect a need for society to broaden collective levels of understanding for those with neurodivergent backgrounds, including doctors. Her letter highlighted problematic societal attitudes and influences when describing how camp counselors treated Grandin. Despite her advocacy and, ultimately, skepticism to fully listen to doctors and camp counselors, Grandin's mother sought guidance from the child psychiatrist and trusted his guidance as a professional, which again highlighted how crucial it is for clinicians to understand neurodiversity. As noted from an excerpt in her letter:

> The same characteristics turn up to some degree in all children, but it is the compulsive quality of her behavior that is the problem. It has also been the point of greatest improvement. When Temple is in secure surroundings where she feels love above all, and appreciation, her compulsive behavior dwindles. Her voice loses its curious stress and she is in control of herself. Difficulties occur when she is tired or when she returns to school after vacation and has to adjust again. Large, noisy groups confuse her. She wants someone near her in whom she has confidence. Her improvement is tied in, I'm sure, with appreciation and love. Until she is secure in her surroundings, knows the boundaries and feels accepted and actively appreciated, her behavior is erratic. (Grandin & Scariano, 1986, p. 44)

Other authors specified helpful supports their parents implemented. Though seemingly small, these everyday actions and supports helped the authors immensely in daily activities. Hall (2001), for instance, described a need for awareness of the daily routine:

> I like to be in charge of things and know what's going on and when it's happening. It is helpful when Mum writes out the day's plans. One thing which

was quite useful was when Mum made me an organizer with a daily schedule. (p. 84)

In some cases, parents had to make great sacrifices in their own personal and professional lives to support their children. For example, Jackson's (2002) mother quit her job so she could homeschool Jackson after being severely bullied at school. Jackson (2002) expanded on her mother's professional sacrifice:

> My mother had to sacrifice her job in order to try teaching me at home, which was a very admirable thing to do considering money has always been a difficult issue for us. . . .
> Those last two years of school were some of the hardest we've ever endured – financially, physically and psychologically. (p. 27)

Parents have to deal with a variety of issues, and some authors described their parents as supportive as possible of them, even in situations not necessarily related to autism. When Prince- Hughes (2004) told her parents she was gay, for instance, her parents tried to find her a place she could meet people with whom to connect:

> As I told them about my feelings, my parents listened carefully and did not make much comment. Soon afterward my mother started driving me down to the nearest city of any size (an hour away) so that I could explore a group run by gay and lesbian people. I had no interest in dating for sexual reasons and still felt that sexuality ran on a continuum. (p. 58)

Adam's story, along with other examples in this chapter, showed regardless of parenting styles, parents' actions had considerable impact on their children's success and access to care.

Furthermore, childhood resentment for not being included in treatment decisions lingered well into adulthood for Adam and certain authors. On the other hand, appreciation for parental sacrifices was also acknowledged during adulthood by some authors. A significant point from this chapter found many authors desired some level of personal autonomy in treatment planning, and medical personnel should include their patients whenever possible.

Differences in Needs: Examples From Education and Employment

Though academic literature related to autistic adults has focused on employment as a main theme of adulthood (Gerhardt & Lainer, 2010), Adam's story and the autobiographies illustrated employment and education were actually settings in which broader themes occurred. Specifically, settings related to education and employment reflected differences in learning and working styles for autistic folks.

- *Contexts*—Authors described different supports pertaining to diverse needs in their places of employment and at schools, ranging from preschool through college.
- *Conditions*—Most often, this category of experiences emerged between teachers and autistic students, or employers and autistic employees. These experiences usually took the form of verbal conversations or the autistic individual being punished by their teacher or employer, resulting in confusion.
- *Interactions*—Several authors described situations in the classroom throughout grade levels in which their teachers punished them for not understanding material or for behaving differently than other students. When they grew older, employers often fired them, not because of unsatisfactory work, but because their social interactions were different than that of their colleagues. Of course, some students actually thrived because they were encouraged by specific teachers to follow special interests and passions, and some adults thrived in their workplaces with the right supports and mentors. Specific examples reflective of different needs are provided in this section
- *Consequence*—For the most part, autistic students and employees were left confused as to why they were being punished, and many seemed to be punished for not conforming to societal norms rather than the actual quality of work they produced. Those who had supportive teachers and employers who understood their strengths and passions, and included them in conversations

related to their needs, were conversely able to find or create an environment in which they could thrive.

Specifically, in employment and classroom settings, it became apparent that autistic individuals have differences in needs and levels of comfort with various modes of communication. For Adam, communicating in sign language was far easier than communicating verbally. By teaching himself sign language, Adam was able to communicate in a way he was comfortable, thus making social connections he otherwise would not have been able to make.

During his time in school, Adam had individualized education programs (IEPs) and was removed from his general classroom to attend a resource classroom; yet, he never knew why he was sent to the resource classroom and felt attending this classroom did not benefit him. He was also not included in the majority of his IEPs, and when he was, he did not feel heard. Just as he was not part of his medical treatment discussions, he was not included in discussions related to his academic support needs. When he was finally allowed to participate in his IEP, however, he was able to write his own behavior contract and address the issue of leaving campus early on many school days. By involving him in the conversation, Adam was able to explain the reason he left school was in response to harassment from bullies. Adam offered to instead call his mom to pick him up if bullying got too intense, and for the remainder of his high school career, he did not run away from school.

In relation to employment, Adam explained because he takes everything literally, he sometimes does not apply for jobs because he feels unqualified unless he meets every single suggested skillset. He also described multiple encounters with colleagues or supervisors in which he took their words literally or was not entirely sure what they were referring to, which resulted in confusion, anger, and sometimes job loss. Over time, Adam learned to focus on his strengths and needs when seeking employment to increase his chance of success. For example, he prefers a quiet environment to work in, as overstimulation by certain sounds cause him headaches and stress. Adam has worked with several job development coaches in the past, and he detailed his experiences, both good and bad, in Chapter Five. Adam also disclosed his diagnosis to multiple employers, and his current employer has been very supportive of Adam following his disclosure. With this employment at General Tools, Adam has been able to find a place of belonging and appreciation for his skills. Like Adam, other autistic authors described similar instances of having diverse needs in the workplace and different ways of conceptualizing information at various levels of education.

Examples From Education

Birch (2003) noted her motivation to learn in school was directly tied to subjects she enjoyed. Because she did not enjoy math, she was not motivated to try. German class was a whole different story:

> In German class we were encouraged to memorize sentences and whole conversations meant that I was, for the most part, more able to converse in German than in English . . . as long as I possessed a stock of sentences which would fit the required topic. Decades later, still unable to talk freely and easily in English, I would return to this foreign language teaching method for the purpose of teaching myself to speak my native tongue! Thus, it can be said that, in some ways, I taught myself English as a foreign language. (Birch, 2003, p. 73)

In some ways, Birch's preference to learn German was similar to Adam's communication preference of sign language, a language he felt more comfortable using.

Blackman (1999) also had certain sensory needs in school, but she was unable to communicate what she needed and did not understand how others experienced sound. As a result, she did not realize what she was going through was any different than her peers:

> Because other people's sounds processing was alien to me, I had no idea that sound should not be like a pressure-cooker lid. I put my hands to my ears for loud sudden noises, but the continuous clamour of everyday life was only relieved by movement I rocked, swayed, and scampered, even though I knew how to sit in one place and that it was expected of me. (Blackman, 1999, p. 51)

Blackman's sensory issues were eventually remedied when she received her ASD diagnosis and moved to a special classroom with a

4:1 student–teacher ratio, ensuring more support for her needs. Grandin also noted in her experiences she felt lost and overwhelmed at her high school, which had 30 to 40 students per class. She was, however, able to find the right environment at Mountain Country School, which focused on strengths and success of each student. She stated, "Being in a smaller school with individual attention made it much easier for me to deal with my problems" (Grandin & Scariano, 1986, p. 61).

Another example of differences in learning needs for autistic students was demonstrated by Dumortier (2002), who described a time when the teacher was explaining something but also made a comment about an open window. Dumortier (2002) could not differentiate between the importance of the educational topic versus the window being open, saying:

> If I need to learn something new, it takes me a great effort to concentrate. Learning anything is much slower for me and takes a lot more time. Doing things also takes longer, demands more attention and requires a much greater effort. Sometimes it seems as if I am not paying any attention when in fact I am. The problem is just that I cannot distinguish between essentials and trivia. (p. 61)

The insight Dumortier provided could be helpful for teachers, who may be able to use this information to differentiate between a student who is not paying attention and a student who simply is not sure which information to which to pay attention. Grandin described a scenario in which she retained information far better when presented in a practical and engaged way that stimulated various senses:

> We saw mummies in the Egyptian exhibits. I was fascinated, visually stimulated, and recounted all sorts of details to my family about this wonderful excursion. But to read about this or other historical events in the social studies book was boring and I'd sit in a corner and escape to my inner world where I dreamed of my magical box which cradled me like warm, loving arms. (Grandin & Scariano, 1986, p. 35)

Several authors experienced school as a frightening and overwhelming place where teachers did not understand them and students bullied them. Hale (2017) described a particularly rough time at school:

> I mostly ignore the teachers. They do not hold my respect and hardly ever say anything worth listening to. The words are not tangible, so have little meaning and therefore are of no use to me. That is, when I can hear what they are saying. Usually they just make garbled rubbishy mush of blurry noises; how do they expect us to understand such weird language? (p. 4)

Prince-Hughes (2004) experienced a teacher who punished her by taking away what she most enjoyed doing, stating,

> My third-grade teacher was not moved by my plight. In general she found me arrogant, insolent, lazy, unpredictable, excitable, and loud. She thought I had been spoiled and that my problems were the fault of my parents. She would assign me more math homework than the other kids (which my father often had to pick up on his way home from work because I missed so much school) and forbade me to focus on the English and reading assignments that I loved. (p. 42)

McKean (1994) had a frustrating experience at the college level; he knew the course content, but flunked because he did not show his work in the way his professor wanted. This lack of flexibility was evidenced in the following passage:

> I moved to Illinois to try some college classes. I flunked out because I did not understand why the teacher wanted us to do things in his own bizarre fashion. I would say to him,
> "Look, if we did it this way instead, we could save four or five lines of code." He said that was true, and it would work but that he still wanted us to do it his way, and that if I did it my way, I would fail. If I was looking for a job as a programmer, I would not have been hired if I used the code he insisted on. I got frustrated from my confusion, failed the course. (McKean, 1994, p. 21)

Jackson (2002) described many factors at school that had nothing to do with academics, yet had profound impact on his school experience:

> When I was in the junior school I had all sorts of problems with bullying, sounds sensitivity (why on earth they have to deafen everyone with a bell, numerous times a day, I will never know!), understanding exactly what I was meant to be doing, forgetting stuff and being too slow at most things. (p. 113)

Bullying was a problem for many authors, including Adam. Shore (2003) described his bullying experiences in school and noted he was even bullied well into adulthood:

> Academics were difficult for me and things were a disaster for me on a social level. Children perceive differences very readily and will blatantly persecute classmates who seem "different." For me, this resulted in much teasing and unpleasantness. I lived in terrible fear of getting "beat up" at the end of every school day. The teachers also thought I was strange . . . I remember my third-grade teacher often telling me that I acted babyish. (p. 53)

Sometimes, no matter how hard she tried academically, Jackson (2002) would still come up short of her teachers' and parents' expectations, noting,

> I try just as hard to learn, I work just as hard, I channel as much effort as I can into my studies – yet it all amounts to the grand total of "what the hell's this? Are you completely retarded?!" This is why I have written this book – to set the record straight about the problems frequently associated with Asperger's Syndrome. (p. 18)

Jackson was homeschooled for the last 2 years of school due to the impact bullying had on academics and her emotional wellbeing. Similarly, Hall (2001) was eventually homeschooled, and did much better when nonacademic challenges of school were removed. As it turned out, he was very gifted in math, but this talent was left unrecognized because other factors, such as noise and crowds, hindered his motivation and ability to work. He noted:

> I didn't do much maths while I was at school because of all the problems like groups and handwriting and boredom and noise. Nobody even knew about my maths gift before Jacinta found out when she did she told the Education Board all about it. (Hall, 2001, p. 60)

Additionally, social needs, such as distress from working in student groups, affected academic performance. Hall (2001) described his struggles in group settings:

> I have a lot of trouble when there are about four or more other children around One difficulty was I couldn't interact properly with a group. It can be hard to be a kid who does not want to be part of any of the groups. (p. 22)

Social issues affecting academic work can be remedied by allowing students the option to work alone or with a single partner rather than a group. Academic accommodations helpful for autistic students include allowing student selection of a preferred seat, assisting in organizational strategies, and having regular interactions to check in with students about non-academic-related stressors (Highlen, 2017). In Hall's (2001) case, he was eventually homeschooled with a tutor, which worked far better for him than the classroom setting in which his social needs were not met, thus interfering with academics. James (2017) felt she was never understood while at school. Rather, she was encouraged to think inside a box both confining and confusing to her:

> Often I can't even see what leaps someone has taken to get to that point. When you look at it from this perspective, you can start seeing autism as an advantage, because we need people to think differently otherwise we'll never make any evolutionary leaps.
>
> Sometimes people on the spectrum can think so far outside the box that it's really important. I'm not sure I was ever praised at school for thinking differently and didn't have a strong sense of belonging. (James, 2017, p. 60)

Other authors noted support and encouragement from specific teachers who took time to understand them greatly influenced their academic success, including Grandin:

> Mr. Carlock, was my salvation. Mr. Carlock didn't see any of the labels, just the underlying talents He channeled my fixations into constructive projects. He didn't try to draw me into his world but came instead into my world. (Grandin & Scariano, 1986, p. 82)

Similarly, Prince-Hughes (2004) said:

> I was amazed when I started fifth grade and my teacher, Kay Eckiss, seemed to understand my problems. She let me complete the Scholastic Reading Achievement tests at my own pace She never criticized my bad penmanship. She allowed me to help start and edit a class poetry journal Best of all, she did not make me go outside for recess and play with the other children. We would have long talks about topics in theology, philosophy, the social sciences, and politics. She wouldn't laugh at me She took me seriously when I said I felt like I was a million years old. The times when she did disagree with me, she gave me reasons. Logical and well-thought-out ones. This separated her from almost everyone else I had ever known. She made me want

to understand. I started to feel like there might be a chance for me not to be alone. (p. 47)

Kim (2015) found acceptance from her Talented and Gifted (TAG) teacher and peers:

> There was Mr. Marek, ready to patiently answer questions with humor and honesty and not an ounce of condescension. He thought we were the coolest kids around and, in that classroom, we thought we were too. TAG was my first hint of what it meant to have a tribe of my own. (p. 31)

As Lawson's (1998) experience illustrated, positive reinforcement can be a far better motivator than punishment for executing academic work differently or outside the box:

> My English teacher there thought I had potential and commented "Excellent work, far above the standard for this class" on one of my essays. I will never forget that teacher because he inspired and helped me to believe I could achieve good work. (p. 55)

In her employment readiness course, Jackson (2002) had a teacher who sought to understand her, thus preparing her for successful employment experiences. She noted:

> I can honestly say there wasn't one aim left untouched. Penny altered the structure of the course around us and our wants and we all benefitted from it ... All throughout the course, we were encouraged to think positively about ourselves, and to focus on what talents we had, rather than the impairments. (Jackson, 2002, p. 108)

Prince-Hughes (2004) had a much better experience in academia when she returned to college to pursue her passion and study behaviors of gorillas:

> The director of research was sympathetic He told me that, with my obvious intelligence and ability to learn without constant guidance, I should certainly be able to study on my own. What I would need was someone to help me when I really needed it and show me how to navigate the system. He agreed to sponsor a series of gorilla behavior research projects. For the next several

years I worked with him, and other helpful people, and was able to apply these studies and my continued zoo involvement toward a degree. (p. 106)

Studying with individuals who understood how positive results can be when education is individualized allowed Prince-Hughes to succeed as a research scientist, eventually completing her doctoral studies. Schneider (1999) also described a positive school experience, in which certain teachers understood his different learning style, thus allowing him to participate in school in a way he could thrive. He noted, "Earlier, I wrote about how I would not take part in the classroom work, but would absorb the material being taught. A few understanding teachers, realizing this, let me sit in the back of the class and draw pictures" (Schneider, 1999, p. 69).

Similarly, Mukhopadhyay (2000) illustrated acceptance and respect from his teachers improved his educational experience and response to instruction. Whereas most teachers and therapists he worked with simply spoke *about* him, rather than *to* him, he described in detail how Ms. Purina took time and consistent effort to build rapport with him, and how developing this relationship of mutual respect and trust helped him to thrive at school:

> I felt very comfortable to communicate with her. I knew I would be accepted. Lady Mathias had brought me to the right person. A person who was not curious about me but who respected me like an individual Soon Ms. Purina could communicate with me.
>
> She was consistent and that helped me not only to sit better in a working environment, but also improve my writing. (Mukhopadhyay, 2000, p. 70)

Shore (2003) also wrote about the ability to connect to people with common interests. He, like several authors, wrote it was easier to converse with adults than peers of his age:

> While middle school wasn't bad, high school was even better. My classmates spent less time being concerned with other people's differences. It seemed that students could move towards specializing in their own interests without fear I spent more time in the music room. I felt comfortable with the older, classically trained teacher. I loved the structure of his music theory class, and he gave me lessons on the trombone during his free periods. I made

friends with many of the teachers. The guidance counselor was a particularly important man to me. I made weekly appointments with him and taught him how to play the flute. (Shore, 2003, p. 85)

Shore also provided insight into techniques that helped him academically:

> Structure in learning is necessary for me to do well in an academic setting. Otherwise I feel awash in an ever-changing sea of data. The structure can either emanate from the instructor or be self-imposed. Having an understandable and coherent structure allows me to create a framework in which I can be creative should the task require that. (p. 90)

Other authors thrived academically, but struggled in other areas. Because Willey (1999) was academically gifted, supports she needed were overlooked. As she described:

> I had received an academic scholarship, admittance into every school I applied to and acceptance into every program I wanted to explore. Objectively speaking, there was no reason for anyone to suspect I needed special counseling of special tutoring or mentoring.
> ... The confusing, rambling, crowded and expansive campus assaulted my limited sense of direction, making it extremely difficult for me to find my way – literally and figuratively – around campus. (p. 50)

Examples From Employment

Adam described taking many sentiments literally, which led to miscommunication with parents and employers. Several authors also recalled taking words literally and reflected on how these misunderstandings influenced friendships, relationships, and employment. Birch (2003) described a tense interaction with a supervisor:

> One day, I had run out of work, so, being conscientious, I kept asking the supervisor if he had anything for me to do. Eventually he got sick of this, and asked me to stop following him around with this question. "Please sit down," he said, "and wait until I find something for you to do." I did as I was told. Some time later, the sales rep came in and demanded "What are you doing sitting there!!!" I felt very hurt and upset, because I had been obeying the rule, yet now the rule seemed to have changed with no warning. (p. 29)

Adam lost his job because of a misunderstanding, and although Dumortier (2002) was a proficient employee, she also continually lost her job due differences in engagement during social interactions:

> I have never really managed very well with colleagues. This is the reason why I keep changing my job or getting fired. Each time I get the same comments, "There are no problems with your work, but we don't know you, you're awkward, you're obstructing the team and your colleagues, nobody can get close to you, you don't anticipate, we have no idea what goes on in your mind." (p. 78)

Others, like Schneider (1999), were denied promotions at work because of perceived personality traits rather than job performance. He noted, "I got my first big promotion at work, my new manager told me that I would have gotten it much sooner, except for the fact that I was considered 'unpredictable'" (Schneider, 1999, p. 106). Williams (1992) was able to give insight on how invasive certain actions can feel. Tapping a person on the shoulder, an action many in society accept socially, may feel overwhelming and intrusive to others. He stated,

> Sometimes the customers would tap me on the shoulder These people had uninvited, tried to take away my choice at being touched, though to them it was a mere tap on the shoulder. These were the people who, out of their own selfishness, would rob me of my sense of peace and security, which, unlike them, I could not find in their version of "everyday life." As people began to explain how other people experienced my behavior, I came to learn that all behavior had two definitions: theirs and mine. These "helpful" people were trying to help me to "overcome my ignorance" yet they never tried to understand the way I see the world. (p. 78)

When Adam began working at General Tool, he was able to focus on his strengths, which led to a sense of empowerment as he recognized other employees depended on him in various ways. Similarly, even after losing multiple jobs, Dumortier (2002) began to understand how her autistic strengths affected her employment:

> My autism is a major trump card in my contact with children and adolescents. All children and adolescents need clarity and structure. This creates

feelings of safety and trust. I am convinced that in some respect my autism makes me an excelled care worker, leader and guide. (p. 102)

With a supportive and appreciative work environment, autistic employees can thrive and contribute invaluable knowledge to their employers. Prince-Hughes (2004) found this at the zoo where she worked for more than a decade, stating,

> I was never so happy. I had to deal with only a few people, usually one on one, and I could spend all my time learning. I did at times have trouble with zoo staff. I was odd and made some people uncomfortable. I had trouble following sequential directions, which was a problem because I was often left alone to complete complicated tasks. . . .The fact that I excelled at certain tasks- keeping records, making keen observations, descriptively communicating information, and memorizing events perfectly—not only saved me but deposited me exactly where I wanted to be. (p. 102)

James (2017) also articulated how autism can positively contribute to employment:

> Autism brings with it many problems, but it also brings many benefits. My ability to zone into one subject and pull out the salient facts quickly and easily is surely something all journalists need. My ability to spot a trend or see a pattern is a necessary skill for every aspect of the work I do. My meticulous need for accuracy – and for all facts to be verifiable – is an important trait for someone who essentially disseminates information. (p. 111)

Conversely, Jackson's (2002) experience showed the right environment in employment is as important as the work itself:

> Found me a placement at the Brentwood Theatre Company. I got on really well there, primarily because the environment was very easy-going and laid-back, with a considerable margin for the sort of social errors Asperger people make. What I mean by this is that, because it was a small company, with crazy, eccentric people like myself, my abnormal behavior was tolerated. This was both a good and a bad thing. (p. 108)

Schneider (1999) was also able to find a perfect fit for his employment with a suitable mix of his strengths, interests, and specific needs, such as working alone. He noted,

> In that organization, I possessed a unique skill, and everybody, from the platoon leader on down, depended on my expertise for that unit's effectiveness. I was a one-man band doing this, and was not a member of any of the gun crews. This dovetailed perfectly with my predilection for doing things in a solitary manner. (Schneider, 1999, p. 61)

Willey (1999) also found enjoyable employment based on her strengths and needs:

> I do not know if teaching at the college level appealed to me more of the freedoms it gave me, or because it did not require me to make much of a change in the routines I had established as a college student. Everything about teaching college classes was as good as, or better than, the best parts of attending them. I liked the structure of the courses, but also the spare time in between. And I most enjoyed the very casual and temporary teacher-to-student relationships. They were the perfect kinds of friendships for me. (p. 67)

Other authors, including Kim (2015), found refuge in self-employment, where they were able to make their own rules about socially acceptable behavior and did not have to worry about others' rules imposed on them:

> I've been my own boss since I was 19, which has allowed me to decide who I work with and how. That resulted in some rather unusual ideas about socially acceptable workplace behavior my ensuring that I was the one making the rules, I wrapped myself in a cocoon of relative safety. (p. 15)

Willey (1999), who eventually left her job in academia due to stressful office politics, found successful refuge by starting her own business revolving around her passion of riding horses:

> I am now the proud owner of Kirkshire Farm, a stable that boards twenty-eight horses, provides training and clinics for riders. Kirkshire is my safe haven that stemmed from my perseverating interest until it became the place that erases my stress and eases my depression while providing me a place to earn money and socialize with like-minded folks My horse's unconditional love and kindness slowly stitched most parts of me back together. (p. 134)

Shore (2003) noted, for those in traditional employment roles, having a mentor when in a work environment is important. Mentorship often helps with social intricacies of the job:

Whether he knows it or not, I have designated him my mentor. I am very poor at reading subtle social situations. Office politics is full of that. This man helps me decode what is going on and how to act or not act. (p. 3)

Differences in Needs

Several authors noted their motivation to learn was directly tied to topical interest (Birch, 2003; Dumortier, 2002). Others, like Adam, had specific sensory needs but sometimes were not yet able to understand or communicate what those needs were (Blackman, 1999). Some authors were better supported after receiving an ASD diagnosis, understanding their specific needs and having those needs met (Grandin & Scariano, 1986). Like Adam, many authors were bullied at school, and this greatly impacted their academic performance in addition to social experiences at school (Hale, 2017; Jackson, 2002; Shore, 2003). Other authors had teachers who refused to accommodate or even acknowledge their needs, which also led to inferior academic performance and less motivation to apply themselves (McKean, 1994; Prince-Hughes, 2004). On the other hand, some authors described finding teachers who believed in them, encouraged them, or simply accepted them for who they were; in response to these positive relationships, students thrived in those specific classes and experienced higher self-esteem (Grandin & Scariano, 1986; Jackson, 2002; Kim, 2015; Lawson, 1998; Mukhopadhyay, 2000; Prince-Hughes, 2004).

Adam, along with other authors, had difficult encounters during employment due to taking words literally. Some of these encounters even led to authors, including Adam, losing their jobs (Birch, 2003; Dumortier, 2002). Other authors were able to find employment based on their strengths and interests. Once they understood their specific needs in relation to how autism affected them, they were able to excel (Dumortier, 2002; Jackson, 2002; James, 2017; Prince- Hughes, 2004; Schneider, 1999; Willey, 1999).

In both school and work settings, I found there is a necessity for teachers, school administrators, and employers to listen to and understand needs of autistic students and employees and make accommodations everyone can benefit from. These interactions had lasting impact and affected autistic individuals throughout their lifetime, from preschool through employment. When autistic people were included in conversations related to their needs, they excelled. When Adam was finally included in his IEP and created his own behavioral support plan, he was able to create a solution that alleviated his response to being bullied, made his parents feel comfortable with his assured presence at school, and satisfied school employees with being able toh respond appropriately to difficult situations rather than running away. For certain authors, these school and work experiences led to confusion and feeling misunderstood, while other experiences led to feelings of empowerment.

Empowerment

Specific contexts, conditions, and interactions leading to empowerment varied across authors, but feelings of accomplishment and personal autonomy were consistent. The components of empowerment included:

- *Contexts*—Empowering situations included autistic authors teaching themselves skills they needed to be self-autonomous, including living on their own, feeling valued in places of employment, expressing themselves through writing, poetry, or music, or focusing on a special fixation to achieve success in employment.
- *Conditions*—For several authors, empowerment came from understanding their diverse needs through context of their ASD diagnosis, including sensory needs and how these specific needs affected their daily interactions and experiences.
- *Interactions*—For many authors, being able to communicate their experiences with loved ones, especially after receiving their ASD diagnosis, led to understanding and acceptance. Specific examples are included throughout this section.
- *Consequence*—Experiences Adam described throughout his story led to feelings of pride, accomplishment, acceptance, and personal autonomy. Adam stated he felt empowered when able to make his own choices, thus the thematic label of empowerment.

For Adam, empowerment came in many forms. Examples included figuring out how to ride the bus so he did not have to rely on his parents for transportation, teaching himself sign language to communicate in a way he felt comfortable, living on his own to fulfill a lifelong goal, pushing himself to work on employment readiness skills, and ultimately gaining employment in which he felt valued. Although academic sources have addressed the importance of attaining self-autonomy in adulthood (Gerhardt & Lainer, 2010; McKenzie et al., 2017), many have not delved into what these empowering experiences may actually look like for autistic adults.

As with Adam, empowerment for the 20 autistic authors emerged from a variety of experiences and situations. Not surprisingly, many authors used writing as a way to process their experiences and often felt a sense of catharsis when writing. Some of this writing resulted in published autobiographies, whereas others expressed themselves by writing poetry or songs.

Prince-Hughes (2004) said,

> Thus, writing was my salvation Written English is my first language and spoken English is my second. Since I was five years old, I have written all the wonderful and terrible things that I could not bear to share. It was too much to disclose in conversation, with my eyes being seared by another human being's gaze. (p. 26)

Writing and poetry created a sense of catharsis for Prince-Hughes, and this was often reiterated by other authors. Similar to Adam, spoken English was difficult at times. Whereas Prince-Hughes preferred written English, Adam preferred sign language. McKean (1994) also felt a sense of catharsis through poetry, and describing the feeling as, "Poetry is a unique form of writing. It can do something no other form of writing can do. It can express complex emotion in a way that is undeniable and clearly understood" (p. 93). Williams (1992) wrote she used poetry to communicate, noting, "I became fascinated with words and books, and making outside order out of inner chaos" (p. 43). When a topic or medium of communication was one she enjoyed, Lawson (1998) thrived, explaining:

> There are other days when I'm working on an assignment for university and feel happy and very excited. I could write essays all day – they do not bite back at me. The written word has a form all its own. The pen between my fingers feels solid and tangible. It moves with me and allows the symbols of my pain or ecstasy to reveal themselves.
>
> Words express my distress through the pen and onto the paper and back to my mind. I can see them on the paper; they talk to me and help me to make sense of my life I can listen better to the tone of someone's voice when I am not confused by the unwritten words of their facial expressions. (p. 97)

When Blackman (1999) learned to communicate via the Cannon Communicator, she felt an unparalleled sense of empowerment. For the first time, she was able to express herself and communicate in a way others understood. She recalled, "I can remember my feeling of triumph. I was getting a reaction, explaining myself, and trying to make the point that I had been aware of my surroundings for a very long time, all at one hit" (Blackman, 1999, p. 89). Several authors also felt a sense of empowerment after being diagnosed with ASD, finally realizing the reason why they felt different for so many years. After Dumortier (2002) was diagnosed, she attended a course for people with autism and remarked,

> For the first time in my life I felt at home and after the second day I didn't want to leave, because I didn't want to lose that wonderful feeling inside me When I arrived home that evening, I cried for hours and realised I had never before felt at ease and that there had never been a place where I had felt as happy as on the course. I realised that I had never fully understood the word acceptance until now. I knew this special feeling had been lacking all my life and I realised that I had not even noticed something essential was missing. (p. 15)

Dumortier gained acceptance after relating to other autistic people, and with this empowerment came recognition of past isolation.

Schneider (1999) felt receiving the correct diagnosis of ASD and understanding his behaviors through this lens was liberating. He noted,

> People whom I know to care about me have expressed concern about the effect that this realization of my autism has had on me. In particular, they worry that I may have discovered that there is something "wrong" with me.

> Very much to the contrary! It was quite liberating. It was that schizophrenia diagnosis that had made me feel almost subhuman Since that initial discovery, I have learned a great deal about autism, both on my own and in consultation with experts. Each new thing that I found out gave me a deeper insight into what and who I am, and why I do the things I do in the ways that I do them. Far from being disturbed by these insights, this self-knowledge has enabled me to accept myself to a degree that I never have before. (Schneider, 1999, p. 79)

Relatedly, the excitement Slavin (2018) experienced after he quit his job to pursue passions of writing and creating music was evident:

> That afternoon I felt embraced and accepted – a part of something new and exciting. I had found my tribe. And by the end of my exhilarating baptism into the pulsating religion of Black Music, I was completely and utterly hooked. (p. 155)

Some authors, like Prince-Hughes (2004), found empowerment through their employment. Prince-Hughes had wanted to be an anthropologist from a very young age, and once she began working at the zoo, she developed a fixation with gorillas and understanding their behaviors. She studied them in academia and in person, and she attributed this passion for her work with gorillas as ultimately helping her better understand her own behaviors as well:

> Very cautiously, I tried to apply the things I'd learned from the gorillas in social situations A feedback loop took shape: I felt generally more calm in my life because I spent so much time with the gorillas, because they made me feel calm, I was able to watch and learn from them. (Prince-Hughes, 2004, p. 136)

Throughout her book, Grandin discussed a fixation with creating a cattle chute type of device for humans to control the amount of pressure she received when hugged. She explained although she craved certain type of pressure from physical contact, the pressure had to be a very specific amount and type so it did not overwhelm her tactile sensory stimulation. Ultimately, this fixation allowed her to become a world-renowned pioneer in her field. She recognized the importance and significance of her work, noting,

> What started out as just a fixation has turned into a life-long dedication of improving the welfare of farm animals by designing humane equipment and facilities My work on cattle behavior and handling is considered pioneering in my field My tendency to fixate was actually an advantage in this situation. It provided me with the motivation to pursue my interest. (Grandin & Scariano, 1986, p. 129)

James (2017), a journalist, made the courageous decision to write about her ASD diagnosis. She received positive response to her article, as many people messaged her to share their own similar experiences. James also brought up an important point several other female authors also brought up—autistic women present differently than autistic men, yet diagnostic criteria is tailored toward behaviors displayed by men. Thus, autistic women tend not to get support they need. In response to the success of her article, she said, "I feel pleased that my instinct was right: it was a story that needed to be told; autistic women cannot continue to be invisible. We need to be seen and heard" (James, 2017, p. 95). After Slavin (2018) received his autism diagnosis well into adulthood, he noted,

> I stepped out onto a crowded London street in a way I never had before. I was new, and everything around me felt open to fresh interpretation. I wanted to shout loudly to the rush hour traffic: I'M NOT STUPID AFTER ALL. . . JUST DIFFERENT-NOT WRONG, JUST AUTISTIC … ! (p. 296)

For Williams (1992), understanding her diagnosis helped her become more self-autonomous and confident: "I was bathing in the freedom to be me. I had a solid sense of home and belonging within my own body. There would be no more self-abuse. There would be no more allowing anyone else to abuse me" (p. 169).

As with other authors, Jackson (2002) found empowerment in solitary sports. He was able to be part of something bigger while still engaging in activities alone at his comfort level. He described his experience as such: "You are at one with all the other people in the world who do Taekwondo. That's quite a cool concept for me because I am usually alone" (Jackson, 2002, p. 155). For Willey (1999), finding accepting activities for her differences allowed her to flourish:

> I eventually found success in an activity that charmed, interested and fulfilled me. I found the speech and dramatic arts club. I think cultural and performing arts types must be Aspies I found great acceptance among my drama peers, most of whom were extremely tolerant and appreciative of diversities and personal visions. I was able to flourish in such a warm and supportive environment, finding it to be the best place for me to turn many of my AS traits into real and viable assets. (p. 37)

Lesley was a nurse who worked at the hospital where Lawson (1998) stayed. Rather than defining Lawson by her limitations, as many other medical personnel did, Lesley helped Lawson feel empowered by showing her respect, which in turn encouraged her to reach her full potential:

> She chose to give me tasks to do for her If I made mistakes she did not get mad at me, shout or take the task away, but tried to teach me, step by step, how to do it properly. Thirty years later, she is still one of the most significant people in my life Lesley was one of the very few people to show a belief in me as a person, and she was the first to help me want to risk the pain of revealing myself and allowing love to reach me she let me know that I was acceptable and lovable, just the way I was For the first time, someone helped me change my thinking, treated me as worthwhile, and started something new in my life. (Lawson, 1998, p. 49)

Similarly, Grandin described a simple and moving way in which her mom treated her as an equal, thus empowering her to learn to read:

> She improved my reading skills by having me read aloud and sound out the words, and she made me feel grown-up by serving me tea. I realize now that the drink was hot lemon water with a tea flavor, but at the time it was pure, grown-up tea. She helped me educationally and raised my self-esteem. (p. 33)

Mukhopadhyay (2000) referred to himself as having two selves—one, an intellectual, and the other, an identity in which even intellect could not help him control certain behaviors socially frowned upon. He emphasized the value of working with people who were aware of and respected different needs noting, "'Yes, you can do everything if it is taught by someone, who is aware of your difficulties,' echoed his other self, who was ambitious and full of inspiration" (Mukhopadhyay, 2000,

p. 46). In part of a poem she wrote, Willey (1999) reflected on how self-acceptance led to empowerment:

> On any given day, I can be just like everyone else seems to be. Until I remember I do not have to be. The me that I am has finally made friends with the differences I no longer try to hide. (p. 112)

Writing poetry, journaling, and writing songs was a form of catharsis and empowerment for many authors (McKean, 1994; Prince-Hughes, 2004; Williams, 1992). Though past employment experiences caused stress for Adam, he has gained empowerment through the encouragement and support at his current place of employment. Similarly, several authors felt empowered when working in a field they were passionate about, or when they found a work environment conducive to their needs, including ones with low sensory stimulation (Grandin & Scariano, 1986; Prince-Hughes, 2004). Additionally, regardless of setting, when autistic authors (including Adam) were shown the respect each and every person deserves, they were able to thrive and achieve their full potential (Grandin & Scariano, 1986; Lawson, 1998; Mukhopadhyay, 2000).

Understanding One's Own Behaviors Through ASD Diagnosis

In his story, Adam said when he discovered his diagnosis at the age of 12, reading about Asperger Syndrome helped him understand his own behaviors. Throughout his narrative, Adam reflected on how some of his behaviors and experiences could be attributed to autism. Several authors also analyzed their own behaviors through their ASD diagnoses, and described feeling liberated by their autism diagnoses. James (2017), for example, said, "My diagnosis helped me make sense of so many things in my life, including my inflexibility and sensory issues, so it has been hugely useful for me" (p. 150).

Prince-Hughes (2004) felt diagnosis of autism is necessary for an autistic person to truly understand themselves, asserting,

> Only after an accurate diagnosis of autism is made can a person begin to understand why they are the way they are and why they always have been this way; only then can they begin to heal from the past and accept the gifts

they offer the future. The restoration of spirit that I achieved through belonging – first with the gorillas, and then to a group of people like myself at long last – is no different for autistic people than it is for all other people who need companionship. It is this sense of companionship that validates one's experience from afar. (p. 33)

Prince-Hughes also spoke about her belief every person with an ASD diagnosis should be informed of their diagnosis, even as a child, to help them understand their behaviors. She asserted society would label them in one way or another for being different, so having the correct label would be beneficial to understanding these differences. Jackson (2002) also described a diagnosis as a tool for understanding oneself:

When we didn't know and didn't have a diagnosis (or weren't told about it) it was a million times worse than you can ever imagine. If the child you are seeing has one or two boxes of the checklist you are working from still unchecked, then please for the sake of their sanity, tell them or their parents if you have any suspicion that they have AS. After all, as we get older and understand ourselves better, then maybe more and more bits of the AS are not so glaringly obvious. (p. 25)

Kim (2015) explained how not knowing she had ASD had resulted in a sense of shame for not understanding her differences:

Before I knew about ASD and the complex ways it influences my life, I blamed myself for a lot of things – for being overly sensitive, easy to anger, controlling, anxious. I knew that I was prone to emotional breakdowns and periods of withdrawal, symptoms I associated with depression or emotional instability. Though I never sought treatment- probably because they were such a longstanding feature of my life- I knew that these things weren't "normal." As I learned more about autism, I came to understand that growing up undiagnosed can leave us saddled with a lot of emotional baggage. Two of the heaviest loads I've carried into adulthood are a strong need for control and a secret sense of shame. (p. 182)

McKean (1994) wished his family had told him about his autism diagnosis, noting,

I felt confused, frustrated, and scared to death. And that is all I felt. It was really just that simple. I was confused because I had no idea what was wrong with me and why I had these problems I did, and I was frustrated because I did not know what to do about them or how to fix them Why did they not do it? Having that explained to me, I would have at least known what it was I was fighting. And you can't fight something without knowing what it is. (p. 70)

Willey (1999) also wished she had known about her Asperger's diagnosis sooner, admitting:

> I know in my heart and in my head, that if I had owned more AS knowledge ... I would have realized I had a different set of needs and wants that set me apart from many of my classmates, but that never meant I was undeserving or incapable. And most important, I would have asked for the support I really needed. (p. 63)

When Willey did receive her diagnosis, she described it as viewing her life in a new light:

> The storm lifted and the answers that explained who my daughter and I were swirled around us like precious gemstones safely washed in with the tide. At last, I had reasons and explanations so rich and real I could almost touch them. For the first time I had the confidence to discuss openly how difficult it was to figure out what other people were communicating, how sounds seemed to glue themselves to one another so that it was grueling to pick them apart, how sensory cues seemed bound and determined to overwhelm and, most telling of all, how aggressive our tempers could become and how hard it was to restrain impulsive thoughts and actions. (Willey, 1999, p. 117)

Grandin spoke at length about fixations and how this common autistic characteristic should be used as a strength and motivator for autistic people:

> My fixations reduced arousal and calmed me. Too many therapists and psychologically- trained people believe that if the child is allowed to indulge his fixations, irreparable harm will result. . . . Fixations can be guided into something constructive Making a positive action on a particular topic can lead to communication——perhaps isolated communication, but at least a break-through in communication. If properly guided, an autistic child can be motivated by a fixation. (p. 32)

James (2017) also introduced special interests throughout her narrative:

> I have always had intense interests. They could be described as obsessions, but many autistic people feel this is a negative word with bad connotations. They prefer the term special interests. I don't mind obsessions – it's how they can feel to me, all consuming. Others have suffered at the hands of professionals who have tried to curb their special interests and stop them from taking refuge in them. So I can see why it is contentious. . . .
>
> Autistic special interests are often also a safety net. Being able to escape into something we love protects us from the harsh and confusing outside world. (p. 63)

Kim (2015) explained the difference between an autistic special interest and a general interest: Like much of what differentiates an autistic trait from a simple personality quirk, the answer is the degree to which the trait is present. For example, when I took up running, I didn't just go out and job a few times a week. I read books about training for marathons. I found workout plans online and joined a training site to get personalized drills Ten years later, I spend more on running clothes and shoes than on everyday clothes If I go on vacation, I pack all of my running stuff. I don't just like to run occasionally; running is an integral part of my life. (p. 98)

Dumortier (2002) spoke of the positive impact her diagnosis had on relationships with her friends and boyfriend:

> The diagnosis has actually helped to save other relationships with friends and acquaintances. . . . The diagnosis gave us an explanation. When they heard about the diagnosis they told me that it had opened up a new world to them, and that before they hadn't been able to get on with me nor had they understood how I felt and thought. (p. 9)

James (2017) described the experience of being diagnosed as an adult with ASD through an exchange she and her husband had when discussing her diagnosis:

> "I just feel as if all my life I have thought I am a dog and have now been given the bombshell news that I am actually a cat." . . . "I don't know which bits of my personality are down to the autism and which bits are inherently me." (p. 17)

When Lawson (1998) told her family she had been diagnosed with autism, she received support and understanding from them, which empowered her to be herself. She noted,

> Recently, I have been able to talk to my family about why I appear so "distant," "scatty," "forgetful" and "unemotional." I explained it is not that I do not have emotions, but rather that I connect with them differently and for different reasons than they do. When I explained my condition, my family was shocked and surprised. They now understand me better and I am free to be myself. Their understanding has freed me from unrealistic expectations. (Lawson, 1998, p. 15)

Kim (2015) explained routines are very helpful for autistic people:

> Routines are a basic survival mechanism. Because autistic people have impaired executive function, planning and decision making can be a big drain on our cognitive resources. Routines keep us from getting bogged down in the little decisions that other people make effortlessly throughout the day. (p. 91)

Many authors, including Adam, felt their lives made more sense once they received their autism diagnosis (Kim, 2015; Prince-Hughes, 2004). Those who received their diagnosis during adulthood were especially able to reflect and understand past experiences and how they responded to certain events prior to their diagnosis (James, 2017; McKean, 1994; Willey, 1999). Many authors also reflected because of their autism, they had a special interest or fixation of some sort (Dumortier, 2002; Grandin & Scariano, 1986; James, 2017; Kim, 2015; Prince-Hughes, 2004). Once these authors understood their special interests within the context of autism, they were able to use it to their advantage in employment settings, or in hindsight to explain how pursuing certain interests may have led to better experiences in school. For some, receiving their autism diagnosis also led to greater support and understanding from family and friends (Kim, 2015). While many were stunned to initially be diagnosed, most were not surprised by their actual diagnosis. They had felt different their entire lives but were finally able to put those differences into context (James, 2017; Prince-Hughes, 2004).

Sensory Experiences

Many authors, Adam included, described having specific sensory needs that would impact them immensely in day-to-day activities. For example, Adam recognized some of his sensory sensitivities would require him to work at a job without customer-service-related tasks or exposure to loud children. Craft (2018) also described sensory sensitivities making seemingly ordinary events difficult to tolerate at times:

> People with sensory sensitivities, like myself, hear everything at once. There is no mute button. And there is no making the noise stop, beyond earplugs and escape. The other senses work the same. Textures irritate. Smells overwhelm and overtake. Sights hurt. And even the taste of air is unpleasant. It appears there is something about my sensory and processing system that causes me to sense things in the environment in segmented, exaggerated parts. (p. 135)

Dumortier (2002) described how sensory overload affected her throughout her days:

> It is very annoying because it affects me every moment of the day. The world often scares me because all my sensory perceptions enter at once . . . the entire situation is out of control and the best thing for me to do is to extricate myself from that particular situation, because if I don't, I begin to panic or my temper flares up. (p. 31)

Hale (2017) also had a difficult time coping with sensory overload during the day. She described how keeping it together during the day exhausted her to her core:

> Each evening when I return home from work or college it feels as if my brain is going to explode. All day long my brain has been greedily gobbling up and trying to process all the different stimuli. I wish I could switch my brain off and stop it from processing absolutely everything that is around me. It is exhausting, continually processing all the intertwined smells, sounds, tastes, visual things and sensations against my skin. Most of these senses are distorted and give me a misleading impression of "the world." At least at home there are not so many stimuli. Consequently my brain has a chance to finish processing all the bombardment from the day. (Hale, 2017, p. 75)

Prince-Hughes (2004) explained autistic people use order and rituals as a way to cope with overwhelming sensory stimulation:

At this point in my life it was the symmetry of the mechanical that I liked. Things were made to fit together in ways that always made sense, in never-failing patters that had purpose Most autistic people need order and ritual and will find ways to make order where they feel chaos. So much stimulation streams in, rushing into one's body without ever being processed: the filters that other people have simply aren't there. Swimming through the din of the fractured and the unexpected, one feels as if one were drowning in an ocean without predictability, without markers, without a shore Autistic people will instinctively reach for order and symmetry: they arrange the spoons on the table, they line up matchsticks, or they rock back and forth, cutting a deluge of stimulation into smaller bits and with the repetition of their bodies' movements. (pp. 24–25)

Jackson (2002) wore a balaclava to help filter out overwhelming sensory input, noting,

A lot of AS and autistic people try to find things to help them feel secure or even to block out the world. When I was younger, my balaclava was something that gave me great security. I used to wear it twenty-four hours a day, seven days a week It served a purpose. The first thing it did was to shield my ears from some of the noise that went on all day every day. I have very sensitive hearing and this is such a noisy world. The main reason was that I felt safe behind it. It was as if I was somehow watching this confusing world from behind a secure screen and the pressure and tightness of the material around my head and face was like being squeezed constantly. (p. 66)

James (2017) said,

I have sensory issues that can dominate my life. On bad days I feel under endless attack from the smells and sounds of my environment. I feel assaulted by bright lights. I can tell at the front door who has had a bath and what oil they have used The definition of ASD refers to subjects being over- or under-sensitive to pain. My threshold is seriously high. (p. 15)

Adam described using verbal stimming to help regulate emotions and sensory input. Kim (2015) also used stimming in a similar way, explaining:

Stimming as sensory regulation: I stim when I'm anxious. I stim when I'm thinking. I stim when my senses are overloaded. I stim when I'm happy. Stimming is a way of regulating my body and mind. It calms me when I'm over-stimulated and reconnects me with myself when I'm under-stimulated.

> Most of the time, stimming is a subconscious activity; I don't even notice that I'm doing it. When I am conscious of it, it feels good: comforting, calming, soothing, fulfilling. (p. 103)

Shore (2003) also had a unique method of moderating feelings when overstimulated:

> I find that becoming overstimulated from spending too much time on airplanes and sometimes at autism conferences often negatively affects my vestibular, proprioceptive, hearing, and other senses. However, swinging in a suspended hammock calms my senses and allows me to interact more effectively with the environment. (p. 51)

Some authors, including Slavin (2018), described experiencing many different sensory inputs at once, but as individual inputs, rather than an integrated view of the scene in front of them:

> Imagine this: You're in a busy high street. You see the wheel of a car, someone's arm, a reflection from a shop window, a discarded coffee cup. This is my world. A world of unconnected bits of things and dots that cannot be joined. Life, for me, is a random collection of unsettling emotions caused by fleeting picture. None of which relate to each other – or to me. (p. 5)

Similar to Adam, many authors described wanting physical touch, but only in very specific ways. For example, Dumortier (2002) said,

> I have gradually learnt to respond casually to touch, even though it affects me differently . . . It is fine if someone grabs me by the arm firmly, it isn't painful, but if someone touches me very softly or rubs my arm or hand, it really hurts. It is unbearable and consequently makes me unmanageable. (p. 45)

Much of Grandin's story led up to how and why she created her hugging machine, and how her life had been so greatly impacted by desire for a certain type of tactile stimulation. In many ways, this desire was similar to Adam's needs for hugs lasting at least 20 seconds and his use of the snuggle buddies service to fulfill that need. Grandin recalled,

> In the second grade I began dreaming about a magical device that would provide intense, pleasant pressure stimulation to my body I craved tender touching. I ached to be loved-hugged. At the same time I withdrew from

over-touch Wanting but withdrawing There is a balance in teaching the autistic child the joy of touch and panicking the autistic child with the fear of engulfment. (Grandin & Scariano, 1986, p. 28)

When talking about sensory integration, McKean (1994) said,

> It is frustrating when your body does not work like it is supposed to. I think for me the most aggravating problem would be the pressure cravings. If I did not have to put so much of my energy into dealing with this, I could get a lot more done every day. There is a constant, low-intensity pain going through me at all times. Sometimes it is not so low- intensity. (p. 63)

McKean was very similar to Grandin in needing a specific type of tactile stimulation. He also created for himself a device to provide pressure on his wrist, which helped regulate sensory needs. For this device, he used old watch straps, which also made the invention more socially acceptable. As another example, Hall (2001) enjoyed the cozy and tight feeling of a sleeping bag and spent hours every day and all free time in his sleeping bag. Similar to other authors, who reported needing to be hugged in a specific way, Hall's approach provided a different way of manifesting that same secure and cozy feeling. He stated,

> I like to sleep in a sleeping bag at night, which I do almost all the time. Even during the day I like to be in my sleeping bag as much as possible I love it so much. My sleeping bag feels brilliant; it is so cosy. The fabric of it is just perfect. (Hall, 2002, p. 32)

Sensory needs, ranging from sensory overload to sensory cravings, were an essential part of many stories. Adam expressed needing to be huggzed in a specific way for a specific duration, described sensory overload in the form of loud noises, and engaged in verbal stimming to help calm his nervous system when he was overwhelmed. Some authors described sensory sensitivities and, when overloaded by these sensory experiences, would struggle in daily activities (Craft, 2018; Dumortier, 2002; Hall, 2017). One coping method authors used to help process sensory stimulation was using order and rituals, or, in Adam's case, engaging in verbal stimming (Jackson, 2002; Prince-Hughes, 2004).

These insights allow readers to understand ritualistic behaviors, not inherently as a symptom of autism, but as a coping mechanism for sensory overload. Though experiences, contexts, and interactions leading to feelings of empowerment varied, all feelings of empowerment were reflective of acceptance, personal autonomy, and accomplishment. Chapter Eight delves into how we can use findings from this section to better our support services for autistic adults.

Relationships

As with the previous section on Isolation, Adam countered the stereotype that all autistic people prefer to avoid relationships. Relationships consisted of the following components:

- *Contexts*—Friendships and romantic relationships occurred most often in school settings, and sometimes developed into marriage or parenting in the home.
- *Conditions*—Several authors yearned for friendship but were shunned by their peers without explanation. Others created close contact with peers and felt supported and loved. Regardless of what type of relationship was described, at some point in those relationships, most authors came to an understanding that they engaged with the world and their peers differently, and had to figure out what that meant for the relationship.
- *Interactions*—Although the relationships between parents and their autistic children was already examined, this section focuses on specific examples of relationships between friends, romantic partners, and autistic parents with their children.
- *Consequence*—Outcomes of these relationships differed greatly from author to author, but all relationships described had profound impact on authors' happiness, support, and sense of belonging.

Adam, for instance, described his desire for friendships and romantic relationships, and how rejection sometimes led to depression. He also described examples in which people shunned him without sharing reasons why, so he had no way of knowing how he could have behaved any differently. Adam was, however, able to connect with peers he felt comfortable interacting with by attending Deaf events in which he could communicate via sign language. In hindsight, Adam realized he spent a lot of time speaking about himself and his childhood resentments, and this made it difficult for him to make and keep friends.

When not in a relationship, Adam was very resourceful and used a professional snuggler service to get physical contact he needed to maintain his mental health. This form of platonic touch served his sensory needs when he was unable to receive platonic hugs from friends or dates. Adam felt very strongly about his need for touch, which also counters the stereotype autistic people do not like to be touched. Rather, as Adam's experiences highlighted, touch more often needs to be of a specific kind and duration.

In his story, Adam also relayed his first sexual experiences and explained how he was able to engage in safe sex. He detailed his experience with his first sexual partner and their dating successes and difficulties. By coding Adam's experiences, I began to understand autistic adults, just like the majority of society, have a vast variety of needs and desires in relationships. Adam's story detailed his experiences with friendships and romantic relationships. Because other authors also experienced parenthood and marriage, the remainder of this section addresses experiences from friendships, romantic relationships (including dating and marriage), and parenthood.

Friendships

McKean (1994) described the importance of friendship: "I think the thing that has helped me more than anything else, any drug or any form of therapy or any behavior management, is the gentle embrace of a friend" (p. 72). Relatedly, Jackson (2002) described the importance of acceptance:

> To my friends I'm an eccentric and an individual, not a freak, nerd or weirdo. My friends are what real friends should be – caring, considerate, always willing to lend a hang whenever I'm in trouble. Words can't describe how much

I appreciate and love them all and how grateful I am to them for rescuing me from a life of solitude. (p. 79)

Willey (1999) described good friends as ones who just let her be who she was with unconditional acceptance:

> To him I was a friend he liked to do things with, someone to share life with for a while... He never questioned me or criticized me, he just let me be. If only everyone could be that gracious – maybe then, we would not even need a definition for Asperger's Syndrome. (p. 65)

Many authors, including Adam, sought and desired support from friends. In some cases, they were able to make friends but lost them without knowing why. Craft (2018) described losing two friendships; one loss occurred during adulthood, and one was her best friend from college. Similar to Adam's experiences with group events, in which he was uninvited but not told why, both friends suddenly stopped talking to Craft without any explanation. She recalled:

> As an adult I have lost a number of friends due to my behaviors and lack of a friendship manual One very close friend (the tea-sipping-on-the-porch kind, where you spill out your guts and cry in each other's arms), she suddenly stopped returning my emails and phone calls, and then un-friended me on a social network site. No explanation. No closure. No reason. Just erased me from her life. (Craft, 2018, p. 88)

Dumortier (2002) wished for friends so she would fit in better:

> If only I could have had a friend, just one would have been enough. Then I wouldn't have felt so abnormal. The problem was that I did feel abnormal during such encounters. The other children looked at me, knowing full well that I was different. (p. 77)

Lawson (1998) also greatly desired friends, but did not know how to make or keep them, noting,

> Throughout my school years, life was extremely difficult. I was constantly laughed at or teased. Sarcasm, criticism or abuse was a common experience for me but I rarely understood why.... I began to want friends, to share my life with others I understood friendship was valuable and I did not want to be

> different any more. However, I lacked the social skills and the "know how" of friendship building. Most people felt uncomfortable with my egocentric and eccentric behavior. I wanted things to go by the rules – and my rules at that! My clumsy efforts to socialize usually ended in trauma—an experience common to most Asperger's teenagers. (p. 16)

Lawson (1998) eventually made a good friend; she described her relationship with him as, "We could not communicate in any depth, but it seemed enough to be in each other's company, and so the relationship continued" (p. 68). Similar to Williams (1992), Lawson described her best friends as able to be present with each other without societal pressures of interactions. Williams (1992) had described this type of friendship through the sense of wanting connection, but also having interactions potentially different from a neurotypical friendship. She said, "In fact Bryn and I communicated directly very little at all . . . In fact we spoke to ourselves about such things far more than to each other, and simply allowed the other person the privilege of listening in" (Williams, 1992, p. 122).

Some authors described friends who took advantage of them. For example, Birch (2003) said, "I had difficulty making friends, and, after making them, would have trouble maintaining them, or would make an unsuitable friend who would then dominate or bully me, so that I could not escape the relationship" (p. 74). Jackson (2002) also described being taken advantage of as a friend:

> These so called friends were actually only opportunists using me for my devotion and services; so when I couldn't provide them with a new Barbie doll or a pretty gold locket they discarded me. For them I was a product to be used up and thrown away-worthless and ineffectual I refused to accept the impossibility of regaining my lost friends. I'd still phone them and when they would slam the phone down on me I'd just phone them right back (this procedure could happen up to 15 times with each ex-friend). (p. 77)

Kim (2015), who experienced bullying throughout her childhood, became a bully to protect herself. Once she started making friends who had common interests with her, however, she was able to stop being a mean girl:

In high school, I found interests I could pursue together with people who didn't tease me. The other mean girls drifted away one by one. I had fewer friends, just one close friend, but I wasn't so afraid. I no longer needed to wrap myself in the armor of bullying to get through the school day or walk through my neighborhood. (Kim, 2015, p. 28)

Several authors used common interests to develop friendships, including Kim (2015): When I've made friends as an adult, it's always been via a common interest... A common interest not only gives me a starting point for conversations, it creates a ready-made activity for spending time together. (p. 56)

Common interests were also a way for friendships to develop into romantic relationships.

Shore (2003) and his now wife used music as a way to relate and connect. Because she was originally from China, there was a language barrier, but they were able to connect and develop intimacy through the language of music. Shore (2003) noted, "We were brought together via a common interest in music. I thought it was pretty neat that we could communicate with each other via music, another type of language, even though we understood little about each other's spoken language" (p. 103). Many authors also described making a close friend, but not being able to hang out with that friend (or any friends) in group settings. Dumortier (2002), for example, opined,

> Friends in a group are also impossible, as my social skills are too poor. Often I don't even get on well with my best friends if we're in a group. They present far more information than I can process at the time and a large proportion of group interactions pass me by, so I can't join. (p. 79)

Hall (2001) also explained the difficulty of hanging out with friends as a group: "In groups I behave differently. I can't concentrate or be friendly at all. I get distracted easily" (p. 41).

Other authors described pets as their closest friends. Hall (2001), for example, continued to reference his cat throughout his book. He described how his cat was one of his best friends and helped him a lot, noting, "the most important people in my life are my close family including Sandy, my cat" (Hall, 2001, p. 24). Prince-Hughes (2004) also noted an affinity for animals, stating,

> The first and best friends I ever had: a family of captive gorillas, people of an ancient nation. These gorillas, so sensitive and so trapped, were mirrors for my soul as it struggled behind bars, gawked at by the distorted faces of my world, taken out of a context that was meaningful and embracing. Because gorillas were so like me in so many ways, I was able to see myself in them, and in turn I saw them – and eventually myself – in other human people. (p. 3)

Lawson (1998), who craved connection but had difficulty making friends, found solace in her cat:

> Although I was unable to relate to other children with animals it was different. I felt a definite connection with my beloved cat given to me by grandmother on my fifth birthday We were best friends and he always seemed to want to be with me. (p. 28)

Romantic Relationships

Several authors described getting married as a way to achieve normalcy and acceptance in the world. After these marriages began to dissolve, however, they realized marriage was not a fix for differences. Birch (2003) said,

> The thought of marriage was not particularly appealing, but it was what "normal" people did. In order to appear "normal," to others and to myself, I could see no alternatives I had long been desperate to appear, and to be, like other people. This was the magic formula! We set a date. (p. 78)

Similar to Adam, Birch (2003) did not want children, and this ultimately was the final straw in her marriage. She noted,

> After five years, Lindsay and I decided that we had had enough. Lindsay now wanted children, and I knew that I was not the right person to provide them. Still waiting to become "normal," I could see that the "instincts" I needed and wanted were just as lacking as before. (Birch, 2003, p. 81)

James (2017) described her first marriage as trying to achieve a sense of normalcy:

> I suppose one's husband should be supportive, but what if I'm not able to allow anyone to do this for me? What if I am just not cut out for marriage

and, if that's the case, why have I married twice? I married for all the wrong reasons. I thought it would fix me or make me complete A few months before the wedding, I had panicked and had tried to call it off. My parents were horrified. The invitations had gone out. Hats had been bought. And so, on that hot August day, I walked down the aisle hoping against hope that this was the thing that would save me. (p. 77)

James had been married to her second husband for 20 years and had four children by the time her book was written. She was not diagnosed with Asperger's Syndrome until well into her second marriage, and she detailed how her marriage evolved as she and her husband sought to process and understand her diagnosis individually and together.

In her book, Dumortier (2002) detailed how her diagnosis helped her and her boyfriend understand her actions and needs better, thus making their relationship far stronger, whereas before the diagnosis, she said her issues caused a lot of problems in the relationship. She "felt misunderstood and let down. I felt I was so different and that I spoke another language" (Dumortier, 2002, p. 7). Prince-Hughes (2004) also described her successful relationship with her life partner, who valued her differences and was willing to support her needs:

> She laughed at my jokes, listened to me, told me her secrets, and cherished my difference. She did something else, too. As we continued dating, growing closer and closer, she started interpreting human behavior for me. If we would go to a party or overhear a stranger's conversation, I would ask her why something was said or why something was done, and she would tell me. Just like that. If I made a social mistake, she would tell me and explain what I did that was out of place why it was so. (p. 156)

Kim (2015) described her marriage before her diagnosis in a similar manner:

> Before my diagnosis, there was a frequent pattern in my marriage: I would unknowingly do something hurtful, then be surprised when Sang was upset by it. This inevitably triggered a downward spiral, Sang assuming I was being intentionally hurtful – because how could a grown adult not realize that it was hurtful – and me feeling bewildered about what exactly I'd done to cause so much upset. Often these discussions stalemated in a conversational dead end. I would sink into shutdown or meltdown, where my only verbal

response was, "I don't know," and Sang would resort to a frustrated refrain of "I don't understand you." (p. 60)

Willey (1999) asserted she and her husband had communication issues, just as in many marriages, but explained these fights were amplified for her and her husband:

> For the first several years of our marriage, Tom had no idea I was misconstruing his thoughts because, from his perspective, he had been clear and articulate. He was left to think I had just failed to listen to him while I was left wondering why he did not care that he had confused me so. (p. 84)

Once Willey received her diagnosis, however, communication began to change for the better in her marriage. She noted,

> I will directly say to Tom – *I think my AS is confusing me. Please start over and tell me again what you are trying to tell me.* This confession of mine has never failed to help both of us stop the arguing immediately, whereupon Tom can begin his point all over again, but this time with a great deal more care and precision behind his words. (Willey, 1999, p. 87)

Adam discussed the development of his sexual desires and early sexual experiences.

Similarly, Prince-Hughes (2004) described how she developed her sexuality:

> I decided to become the best object of sexual advance that any woman could dream of. I watched erotic videos, read all kinds of manuals, listened to women talk in the dressing room offstage about the things they really liked in a lover, and grilled them about what worked and what didn't when it came to sex with women I drew extensively on the protocols I had compiled to apply my data in successive encounters with women full of desire. (p. 80)

Shore (2003) explained it took 3 years of dating before he was able to explore sexual intimacy with his now wife:

> It wasn't until our third year together that I was able to explore intimate relations with her in the fullest sense of the word. There seemed to be a wall that needed crossing, yet I was unable to figure out what that barrier was. Perhaps the problem was sensory overload.

She must have had a lot of patience, gentleness and a willingness to accommodate differences even if she did not know what they were. (p. 95)

Parenting

Though Adam does not have children, nor a desire to have children, a few authors who are parents described how ASD affected parenthood. Prince-Hughes (2004), for instance, reflected on how her ASD traits were a strength when parenting:

> When my son was born, I sobbed. I had never cried so hard before. I was totally overwhelmed by the love I felt for him In response to the difficulty and unfamiliarity of my new circumstances, I fell back on my habit of structuring. I would wake up at six-thirty and sing to my son until he woke up. (pp. 192–193)

In addition to structured routines to help with parenting, Kim (2015) pointed out when her child had various fixations as a toddler, she was able to home in on them and develop activities around them:

> And when your little boy or girl develops a fascination with butterflies or dump trucks, you can put your Aspie tendencies to work: visits to the library, field trips to construction sites, collecting things! As an Aspie, I'd already mastered one of the keys to parenting a toddler: routine. (p. 77)

James (2017), who has four children, felt motherhood was difficult because processing emotions of her children could be overwhelming at times:

> My experience of motherhood is, I think, in many ways different to that of neurotypical women. As well as not recognizing my own emotions and feeling them at a very muted level, I don't cope well with the emotions of others. I would like to live in a world where we all went along on a straight emotional line, never feeling anything too strongly. (p. 134)

Kim (2015) also felt different from other moms, noting,

> The thing about these playgroups is that the moms are there as much to make friends for themselves as they are to socialize their children. I accepted exactly one play date invitation from another mom. It wasn't a disaster exactly, but it

was a classic case of wrong planet syndrome. The other mom and I had little in common and I didn't have the social skills to bridge the gap. (p. 78)

Kim also compared raising her daughter with a neurotypical husband to growing up in a bicultural household:

> For a neurotypical kid like Jess, it was probably confusing at times. In a way, she grew up in a bicultural household, and like many children from multicultural families, she learned to intuitively translate between autistic and neurotypical. (Kim, 2015, p. 84)

Finally, Willey (1999) recognized her differences as a mom, but emphasized, despite what professionals and parenting books may suggest, there is no one right way to parent:

> I realized early on, way before I heard the words Asperger's Syndrome, that I reacted to the world in unusual ways, but I never told myself this would mean I could not become a loving and good mother. I was not put together like other moms, but I was still my daughters' mom and I was determined they would have the kind of care they needed from me. I soon learned to put the parenting books away when I came across passages that seemed to suggest there was only one mom, only one way to love a child. (p. 103)

The experiences highlighted in this section reflected many autistic adults desire relationships of some sort. Some crave friendships while others pursue romantic relationships. Some are successful relationships, and others are unsuccessful. Contrary to stereotypes autistic people are to blame for failed relationships due to social differences, the unsuccessful relationships were more often due to a mutual lack of understanding by the autistic authors and their peers or romantic partners.

Conclusion

Chapter Seven explored in detail the thematic categories derived from both Adam's lived experiences and the 20 autobiographical accounts. The coding of Adam's story combined synergistically with the autobiographical constant comparison model and led to the following categories and subcategories: Isolation (Mental Health, Societal Expectations, Medical Treatment and Diagnosis); Influence of Parents; Differences in Needs: Examples from Education and Employment; Empowerment (Understanding One's Own Behavior through ASD Diagnosis; Sensory Experiences), and Relationships (Friendships, Romantic Relationships, Parenting).

Although the authors' experiences might have emerged differently within each category, all experiences aligned with each category had common components, which I explained in each section. These codes and themes are then further explained by theories, old and new, which allow for a more thorough understanding of setting, contexts, and participants. These theoretical foundations are also critical to predicting and explaining human actions (Saldaña, 2016). Chapter Eight explores the two main theories that stemmed from my themes: neurodiversity paradigm and monotropism theory.

Chapter Eight

Findings

In the final stage of grounded theory analysis, researchers must "address the 'how' and 'why' questions to explain the phenomena in terms of how they work, how they develop, how they compare to others, or why they happen under certain conditions" (Saldaña, 2016, p. 251). The central underpinnings of this study held that autistic adults have diverse experiences and needs not currently met by society, and the two proposed theories to address and understand this phenomenon are the neurodiversity paradigm and monotropism theory. Although neither theory is new, they remain strikingly underused in education or psychology fields. Chapters 8 and 9 help explain how society can understand autistic behavior through a combination of the neurodiversity paradigm and monotropism theory and use this understanding to modify our own behavior and create a more inclusive environment for the diverse needs of autistic adults.

From the social model of disability, a group of autistic individuals developed the neurodiversity paradigm, which reiterated autistic brains simply contain ordinary variations found in humans (Angulo-Jimenez & DeThorne, 2019). The paradigm emphasized understanding autism as a difference, not a disorder. This paradigm also stressed many challenges people with ASD face can be alleviated by environmental changes rather than focusing on neurological differences (Angulo-Jimenez & DeThorne, 2019; Jaarsma & Welin, 2012). Another theoretical framework rooted in the social model of disability is monotropism theory. This theoretical framework humanizes the diagnostic criteria of ASD, but it has largely been ignored in academic and medical fields (Murray et al., 2005). Both theories encourage understanding lived experiences of autistic people through the social model of disability. The social model of disability also emphasizes the influence of social, political, and cultural contexts without denying physiological aspects of impaired functions (Baglieri et al., 2011; Siebers, 2011).

This understanding of disability was illustrated in the autobiographies; after all, the decidedly different time periods the authors wrote about reflected different societal and cultural attitudes toward autism, and toward disability in general. Authors of earlier autobiographies mentioned psychologists alluding to refrigerator mothers as a cause of autism and doctors primarily recommending institutionalization. Even the authors themselves tended to write about their autism as something to be fixed. On the other hand, the authors of autobiographies published from 2010 onward tended to use the terms neurodiversity or neurotypical and largely spoke about their experiences of autism as a difference to be understood rather than a disorder to be fixed. These evolving social constructs of autism have the potential to be further understood using the neurodiversity paradigm and monotropism theory, both of which were created and supported by neurodivergent scholars (Chown, 2020).

Neurodiversity Paradigm

It is important to understand and explore different ways to talk about autism because labels impact a person's sense of identity. Language associated with a topic gives it meaning and, currently, the majority of discussions revolving around autism use language of neurotypical people rather than neurodivergent people (Chown, 2020). In their book, *Neurodiversity Studies: A New Critical Paradigm*, Rosqvist et al.

(2020) defined neurodiversity as, "perceived variations seen in cognitive, affectual, and sensory functioning differing from the majority of the general population or 'predominant neurotype', more usually known as the 'neurotypical' population" (p. 1). Neurodiversity studies have been informed by sociology, critical psychology, critical medical humanities, disability studies, and critical autism studies. According to Walker (2014), most studies of autism describe autism as a deficit rather than simply a "diverse way of being" (p. 1).

Rosqvist et al. (2020) specified neurodiversity should be applied to a group, not individual people, because diversity is a trait possessed by groups. Neurodiversity refers to both neurotypical and neurodivergent people, or multiple groups of neurodivergent people. neurodivergent refers to a person whose brain differs from the societal norm. Sharing a form of neurodivergence can be referred to as neurominority in lieu of people with disorders, which contributes to oppression and exclusionary medical, social, and economic practices. Even in neurodiversity there are differences, and even within one neurotype, such as autism, there are differences (Hillary, 2020). Chown (2020) asserted autism can be understood as a combination of neurological differences and societal oppression. In line with the social model of disability, neurodivergence is a path to depathologize biopsychosocial differences perpetuated by predominant medical and cultural models (Rosqvist et al., 2020).

Essentially, neurodiversity strives to recognize autism as a form of divergence rather than a deficit, which will better allow therapists and academics to support autistic people to reach their full potential (Rosqvist et al., 2020). Neurodiversity can be thought of as a neurocognitive variation, but as a term, it does not hold negative connotations and does not have to imply medical pathology (Chapman, 2020). According to Robertson (2010), though every autistic person has their own set of needs, autism creates variation in cognitive strengths and weaknesses in the following four categories: language, communication, and social interaction; sensory processing (environmental input); motor skill execution (environmental output); and goal-oriented and reflexive thinking, planning, and self-regulation. The ubiquity of these themes was also reflected via common themes throughout Adam's story and the 20 autobiographies.

Although the authors' experiences were often very different, themes reflecting these experiences were similar. Within the neurodiversity paradigm, researchers and clinicians have acknowledged these commonalities in neurotypes, but have strived to focus on individual strengths of autistic people rather than perceived deficits (Robertson, 2010).

Research in academia, as well as medical practices, is currently dominated by the medical model, which reflects the neurotypical perspective. Practices based on the medical model are tailored to help individuals live independent, social, and economically productive lives. These practices reflect a drive to cure or fix perceived deficits, which are defined by cultural and social ideals. Neurodiversity counters the deficit model and counters the need for a cure; instead of emphasizing neurological differences as part of one's identity, it emphasizes the need for neuroequality (Rosqvist et al., 2020). As Robertson (2010) noted:

> Another important facet of the neurodiversity perspective is its recognition that difficulties experienced by autistic people are always contextual. The neurodiversity perspective contends that living in a society designed for non-autistic people contributes to, and exacerbates, many of the daily living challenges that autistic people experience. . . Sensory demands, social ambiguities, and information complexities are among the barriers that the modern 21st century presents to autistic people. (p. 3)

Neurodiversity is a subset of the social model of disability because it focuses on lived experiences to help society understand barriers autistic people face in social and cultural worlds. By including autistic people in research design, implementation, and support services, academics and therapists can learn from neurodivergent people about problems that the social and cultural worlds present them with, thereby moving toward a more socially just society.

Hillary (2020) compared differences in neurocognitive communication to differences in cultural communications. She stated learning from autistic autobiographies is akin to learning about cultural practices of a neurotype. Walker (2014) echoed this sentiment, saying:

> The idea that there is one "normal" or "healthy" type of brain or mind, or one "right" style of neurocognitive functioning, is a culturally constructed

fiction, no more valid . . . than the idea that there is one "normal" or "right" ethnicity, gender, or culture. (p. 1)

Similarly, in her autobiography, Kim (2015), who was neurodivergent and whose husband was neurotypical, described her daughter as growing up in a bicultural household. Too often, a difference in perception or experience is blamed on the neurodivergent person's social deficit, when in fact it is the responsibility of both parties to try to understand each other's behaviors and communication style. For example, theory of mind is often used to explain that autistic individuals cannot put themselves in someone else's shoes; however, inverting this theory asserts we as neurotypicals cannot understand mental processes of neurodivergent people (Leong, 2016). In his autobiography, Hall (2001) said, "Normal people should try harder to understand AS people because AS people have difficulties with some things most people find easy" (p. 98).

Differences between expressions of autistic neurocultural practices and neuronormative western cultural practices were apparent in the autobiographies, especially in the theme of Societal Expectations. In that theme, several authors were quoted trying to understand what the neurotypical concept of "normal" social behavior actually entailed. Storytelling and narratives helped provide understanding on goals behind neurodivergent people's actions, allowing society to learn about a different value system rather than simply assuming the behavior is due to autism (Hillary, 2020). Due to an existing culture of ableism, however, differences of neurodivergent people are often pathologized and encouraged to change to neuronormative preferences. Milton (2012) referred to this phenomenon as the double empathy problem:

> A disjuncture in reciprocity between two differently disposed social actors which becomes more marked the wider the disjuncture in dispositional perceptions of the lifeworld – perceived as a breach in the "natural attitude" of what constitutes "social reality" for "non-autistic spectrum" people and yet an everyday and often traumatic experience for "autistic people." (p. 884)

The current acceptable explanation for differences in behavior is autistic people's behaviors reflect deficits, and the acceptable form of treatment is to encourage autistic people to modify behaviors to reflect mainstream cultural norms and expectations. Milton's (2012) double empathy problem reconceptualizes the problem as a mutual lack of understanding of other's behaviors by neurodivergent and neurotypical people, and the appropriate form of treatment would be to work toward understanding these dichotomous behaviors. Another way to understand why people act for reasons different from our own is to use stories (Hillary, 2020), such as Adam's narrative and the autobiographies examined in this study.

Stenning (2020), who researched autistic life writing, categorized three generations of autistic life writing based on time periods and DSM criteria during those periods. Understanding different experiences based on these time periods reflects the social model of disability by taking into account how differing social norms of each time period were represented in the authors' writing styles and life experiences. The first time period reflected writings from 1987 to 1993, which was when the first version of the DSM was used that included ASD diagnosis. These authors mostly presented their lives in chronological order and focused on explaining what autism was, mostly from a medical model perspective. Their attitudes reflected one could live a good life, even with autism. These earlier autobiographies were largely questioned by professionals because it was not accepted that autistic people had the intellectual ability or capacity to reflect on and write about their own lives (Stenning, 2020). As described in Part One of this book, Temple Grandin's foreword was written by Dr. Bernard Rimland, a research psychologist who had a son with ASD (Grandin & Scariano, 1986). In the foreword, Rimland expressed doubt Grandin had autism based on her ability to communicate clearly with him, which reflects the stereotype people with autism are not as competent as their neurotypical peers.

The second generation of life writing was based from 1994 to 2013, and was written after changes to DSM-4 (1994) were published. This iteration included ASD and Asperger Syndrome as two separate diagnoses and established the onset of ASD no longer had to be before 30 months. These autistic life writings were considered quest narratives, in which adults reflected on their lives and what it meant to have ASD (Stenning, 2020). These books reflected the autism self-advocacy movement and questioned pathology of autism while encouraging autistic individuals' voices to be central to understanding autism. The Autism Self-Advocacy Network also encouraged the philosophy of "nothing about us without us." This rallying cry helped give voice to autistic individuals as they sought to prove, despite differences in social, communicative, and sensory expressions, they did not lack ability to relate to others (Stenning, 2020).

The final generation of autistic life writing was written after 2013. This era occurred following DSM-5 (2013), when Asperger Syndrome was no longer listed as a diagnosis. This category of books moved toward a "socially situated understanding of autism" (Stenning, 2020, p. 115). Similarly, the autobiography authors of this time identified autism as a key part of their identity, rather than a medical condition. These books could possibly be considered autoethnography. Though the authors reflected a moral capacity and ability to narrate these thoughts and experiences, individuals with autism have continued to be questioned on their empathy and ability to relate to others (Stenning, 2020).

The three generations of autistic life writing reflect understanding of ASD, and related empathy skills and moral capacity, has as much to do with readers as the writers. Autistic authors have clearly demonstrated their ability to articulate and experience empathy, theory of mind, and relatability to others, but readers may still interpret those experiences as a deficit or as something to be overcome. It is not the responsibility of the writer to meet expectations of reader; rather it is the responsibility of the reader to receive information with an open mind. For this reason, it is critical to read and learn from autistic voices without preconceived notions of the medical model. Understanding and expanding upon the neurodiversity paradigm provides an important viewpoint that counters the medical model and allows purer appreciation of viewpoints and the autistic experience. Through this lens, autistic individuals are also able to own their own narratives and describe their experiences in language not rooted in the deficit medical model approach society has continued to depend on.

One strategy to reconceptualize autism from the preexisting deficit perspective to a neurodiversity perspective is to understand sensory experiences of people with autism as they explain these experiences,

Table 2. Neurodiversity Paradigm

Deficit Model: DSM	Social Model: Neurodiversity Paradigm
Persistent deficits in social communication and social interaction	Diversity of human minds, the infinite variation in neurocognitive functioning within our species
Deficits in social-emotional reciprocity	Neurodiversity is a natural and valuable form of human diversity.
Deficits in nonverbal communication	The idea there is one "normal" or "healthy" type of brain or mind, or one "right" style of neurocognitive functioning, is a culturally constructed fiction, no more valid (and no more conducive to a healthy society or to the overall well-being of humanity) than the idea there is one "normal" or "right" ethnicity, gender, or culture.
Deficits in developing, maintaining, and understanding relationships	Social dynamics that manifest in regard to neurodiversity are similar to social dynamics that manifest in regard to other forms of human diversity (e.g., diversity of ethnicity, gender, or culture). These dynamics include dynamics of social power inequalities and also dynamics by which diversity, when embraced, acts as a source of creative potential.

rather than assuming autism is something to be pathologized (Jackson-Perry et al., 2020). Because voices of autistic individuals are not often included in research or dialogue related to autism, sensory experiences are pathologized rather than understood as a neurodivergent form of communication. Jackson-Perry et al.'s (2020) concept was acutely illustrated by the entire theme of Sensory Experiences from Adam's story and the autobiographies. Nearly every author described some sort of sensory need and gave myriad explanations for their sensory experiences or sensory-related behaviors. Cocreating knowledge alongside autistic adults will allow for a deeper understanding of autistic life experiences and help challenge stereotypes and current societal understandings of ASD, which are rooted in deficit discourse.

The neurodiversity paradigm, a subset of the social model of disability, is a lens through which we can depathologize disability and think about function and dysfunction in a different way. Neurodiversity challenges the idea of a normal cognitive style and emphasizes, instead, it should be the norm we all function differently (Chapman, 2020). Throughout thematic examples presented in Chapter Seven, neurodiversity was illustrated by the authors' experiences, admittedly unique ways of processing information, and diverse outlooks on the world. Due to the nature of neurodiversity, its definition is ever evolving and will mean different things at different times. As Chapman (2020) noted:

> Neurodiversity is likely what philosophers call a 'moving target', meaning that the concept will continue to change and 'move' due to complex interactions between those who are categorised by it (including both neurotypicals and neurodivergents), as well as the various relevant institutions it challenges and responds to (psychiatry, education, etc.). (p. 219)

The neurodiversity paradigm is more than an academic concept. Though it helps foster understanding of difference in ways that contrast with the medical model of disability, actually using the neurodiversity paradigm will help facilitate increased empathy for people of all differences, create collaborative approaches to research and treatment designs, create societal spaces in which everyone is welcome, and create a shared language in which to express a difference without pathologizing it. Ultimately, these improvements could lead to real societal change.

Monotropism Theory

For society to develop a complete understanding of autism, society needs to hear from those with autism and include autistic individuals in research designs, implementation, and theory building. Monotropism theory was created by neurodivergent authors in response to autism diagnostic criteria in the DSM, and has been well supported by autistic people, who feel it more accurately captures the meaning of autism than the DSM's diagnostic criteria (Chown, 2020). Throughout the changing criteria for ASD via the DSM and International Statistical Classification of Diseases (ICD-10), one consistent factor was autistic people used "atypical strategies for the distribution of attention" (Murray et al., 2005, p. 139). The authors believed, "The 'restricted range of interests' referred to in the third part of both sets of diagnostic criteria, which we call monotropism (Murray, 1992), is central to the autistic condition" (Murray et al., 2005, p. 139). The authors of this theory asserted,

> Our hypothesis is that the difference between autistic and non-autistic is a difference in strategies employed in the distribution of scarce attention. That is to say, it is the difference between having few interests highly aroused, the *monotropic* tendency, and having many interests less highly aroused, the *polytropic* tendency. An aroused interest is an interest charged with feeling. (Murray et al., 2005, p. 140)

Monotropism highlights different cognitive processes people employ to focus their attention. Murray et al. (2005) explained some people are able to distribute attention across many different interests whereas others concentrate their attention on a few interests; sometimes leading to competition between mental processes for attention on a specific topic.

Activities such as social interactions, shifting attention from one thing to another, and using language are all examples requiring attention to be broadly distributed. These activities are difficult for autistic people, who typically pay attention to a few topics of interest to them (Murray et al., 2005). Those who are monotropic may have trouble tending to tasks not perceived as valuable to them, specifically because their attention resources are focused on other tasks with personal value. Essentially, monotropic people possess capacity to focus very well on a task so long as that task is valuable to them. Top-down processing is difficult for monotropic individuals because their interests create a sense of definite knowledge, and with this knowledge comes expectations about the world. When these expectations are contradicted or changed, distress may ensue. Thus, top-down processing, which requires an individual to use previous information and apply it to a current situation, is difficult, because the majority of information for a monotropic individual is related to their narrow range of interests. On the other hand, monotropic individuals are able to retrieve a plethora of information related to their narrow range of interests (Murray et al., 2005). Along the autism spectrum, people have different ways of thinking, mostly influenced by monotropism and what is deemed relevant to each person, but there is also general bottom-up processing. This processing is different from neurotypical processing, which usually entails confined thoughts to a preconceived conceptual framework (Rosqvist et al., 2005). This difference in processing allows for a different set of perspectives and ways of experiencing events, making it crucial to listen to autistic voices.

Murray et al. (2005) explained neurotypical language does not usually speak about experience in terms of sensory experience; namely, what these experiences meant or what inferences were drawn from collection of sensory experiences. This difference in language makes it difficult for someone with ASD, who might primarily experience sensory input without the attached social inferences to explain those experiences. One common saying is, if you have met one person with autism, you have met one person with autism; this means there is so much variability along the autism spectrum there is no common picture of what autism looks like.

Murray et al. (2005) posited this variability is because of monotropism. Those on the spectrum have different levels of skillsets based on their narrow range of interests and how those interests may have been used to learn various skills. According to monotropism theory, individuals can perform a range of tasks very well so long as an understanding of the topic and a motivation to complete the task are present (Murray et al., 2005).

Monotropism is also responsible for restricted, repetitive, and stereotyped patterns of behavior outlined in the DSM criteria, and this behavior may lead to thoughts and actions repeated over and over again (Murray et al., 2005). Due to a narrow attention tunnel, unrelated information might not even be processed. Additionally, making connections or inferences outside of monotropics' range of interests is difficult and might take time, though creating these connections in their range of interests is often quick. Murray et al. (2005) noted, "I cannot 'move on' unless certain ritualistic expectations are met (meals, words, events). At times, even though specific things have been told to me, I lose the feeling of their reality and am desperate to know them again" (p. 146). For those with monotropic tendencies, it is difficult to anticipate changes unrelated to their interests, which may create feelings of dread, hopelessness, and lack of safety when confronted with change or an unexpected event. It is also difficult to relate to others or understand others may not have the same monotropic interests. It is often easier to relate to those who have similar monotropic interests, as was evident in the autobiographies when several authors described using their special interests as the basis to make friends.

Practitioners largely understand, due to monotropism, people with autism may not take in other contexts to understand a situation. Murray et al. (2005) expanded on this idea:

> We tend to focus upon one thing at a time and this might mean we "miss" lots of superficial information that gives context to much of life (conversation, expectation, realization). However, when one understands this, it should make relating to us less troublesome. (p. 152)

Emotions and judgments may be extreme due to viewing situations through the monotropic tunnel, but using the attention tunnel to motivate someone to learn various skills may be an effective strategy for adding meaning to tasks. Motivation comes from emotional reward and recognizing a person's motivations and interests is critical to supporting those with ASD (Murray et al., 2005).

Monotropism theory can also be used to understand many aspects of autistic experiences.

Stenning (2020) addressed a common misconception about autistic people, which is autism causes deficits in empathy and theory of mind. This stereotype inaccurately implies people with autism are not fully moral. Stenning explained lack of empathy for many people equates to a lack of sound moral judgment, and consequently, those with ASD are often not believed in their experiences. When looking at empathy and theory of mind through the lens of monotropism theory, however, and the ability to have intense focus on one topic, autistic people may in fact have greater capacity to create impactful social change. For example, Greta Thunberg flipped the logic autistic people lack empathy by claiming, because those with ASD are allegedly not bound to social norms, this freedom may in fact allow them to have a superior capacity for moral judgment, as no outside source can influence their moral compass (Stenning, 2020). Rosqvist et al. (2005) corroborated this with Seng's theory, which asserted those with autism process information in a less biased way, as they are not bound to, or as influenced by, societal influences:

> An autistic person's exploration of the world is therefore more unconditional, less prejudiced, since the person is not strongly bound to the concept world and thus does not process sensory information according to predetermined concepts and framings to the same degree as neurotypical people. Autistic people approach the world as phenomenologists and proceed more from what the senses say than from learned interpretation patterns. (p. 157)

Monotropism theory was woven into every single autobiography in some way and was duly reflected by quotes from every theme. Several authors described applying themselves at school and excelling in subjects they were interested in or passionate about, while failing or bored in subject matters that did not interest them. For example, Birch (2003) said,

> My love of books and of language meant that, on entering my school years, I was keen to learn reading, writing and spelling, and was always at the top of my class in these subjects. Following on from this, my written work was excellent. This contrasted with my poor ability, and lack of interest, in mathematics. (p. 93)

For Grandin, monotropism was used as a powerful motivator to learn:

> My fixation had been channeled into something constructive and aroused my interest in science. Obsessed by solving the Distorted Room puzzle, I began to study some of the boring subjects just in case I might learn some things that would really interest me. (Grandin, Scariano, 1986, p. 80)

Prince-Hughes (2004) was also able to use her fixation to her advantage at an early age when she learned about anthropology, noting,

> When we began to have social studies and I learned about anthropology, I was fascinated with early humans and knew that I would be an anthropologist

Table 3. Monotropism Theory

Deficit Model: DSM	Social Model: Monotropism Theory
Restricted, repetitive patterns of behavior, interests, or activities	Different cognitive processes and strategies people employ distribute of scarce attention.
Stereotyped repetitive motor movements, use of objects, or speech	"Much of autistic behaviour can be seen as attempts to restore some kind of equilibrium. 'Restricted, repetitive behaviours' are a natural response to feelings of instability. They allow you to assert control over what is happening, and feel safer. This is probably a useful general rule, not something that's only true in autism – we see restricted, repetitive behaviours in all sorts of contexts, it's mostly just that autistic people's ones stand out as particularly odd, to most people" (Murray, 2019, p. 47)
Insistence on sameness, inflexible adherence to routines, ritualized patterns of verbal or nonverbal behavior	Because of the narrow attention tunnel, unrelated information might not even be processed.
Highly restricted, fixated interests that are abnormal in their intensity or focus	Those who are monotropic may have trouble attending to a task that is not perceived as valuable to them, specifically because their attention resources are focused on other tasks that do hold personal value
Hyper- or hypo-reactivity to sensory input or unusual interest in sensory aspects of the environment	Neurotypical language does not usually speak about experiences in terms of sensory experiences, but rather what these experiences meant or what inferences were drawn from the collection of sensory experiences. This difference in language use makes it difficult for an autistic person, who might primarily experience the sensory input without the attached social inferences, to explain their own experiences

someday. I practiced on the playground: I would make willing children lie still on the ground so that I could "discover" their remains. I would act out the stages of evolution. I would run around the playground with a notepad and ask people why they were doing things. This was something I could really understand. After all, anthropologists lived among those whose ways of being were totally foreign to them in order to learn more about their culture. (p. 46)

For Grandin, Prince-Hughes, and several authors, their fixations ultimately led them to successful careers as they used their special interests and related skills to excel in their given fields.

To address diversity of needs across the autism spectrum, Tables 2 and 3 use the neurodiversity paradigm and monotropism theory to present an alternative way of understanding autism. This model reflects what is currently used to understand autism, the deficit model, and what can be used instead by researchers, teachers, therapists, and medical professionals to better support their neurodivergent clients. It should be noted that these tables are meant to present alternate theoretical frameworks for understanding autism, and the social model portion of the table may not align with an exact replacement of the current diagnostic criteria, especially since the diagnostic criteria usually changes with each new DSM edition. Additionally, the information in these visuals help humanize behaviors and experiences of autistic individuals to ensure a better quality of life for autistic adults. Schalock (2000) defined the eight core components of quality of life as self- determination, social inclusion, material well-being, personal development, emotional well- being, interpersonal relations, rights, and physical well-being. Specific actions teachers, service providers, researchers, medical professionals, and society can use to be more inclusive are outlined in Chapter Nine.

Chapter Nine

Discussion and Conclusion

This research study explored the lived experiences of autistic people to better understand their needs as they transition to adulthood. I executed this study by directly speaking to someone on the autism spectrum and simultaneously examined autobiographies, memoirs, life histories, and literature produced by autistic adults. My objective was to disseminate information that expands upon existing literature on how to best support autistic adults as they navigate complexities of adulthood. This research used the social model of disability and first-person perspectives to offer a different understanding of experiences, needs, supports, challenges, hopes, aspirations, and services for autistic adults as they transition to adulthood. Additionally, by reading autobiographies of autistic adults as part of the literature review and data analysis, this study ensured autistic voices were central to discussion related to autistic needs. The insights gained directly from Adam and the other authors often highlighted the role society plays in perpetuating notions of disability and led to my use of the neurodiversity paradigm and monotropism theory to help society better understand how to create inclusive environments for the neurodivergent. This final chapter outlines my original research questions and findings related to each question, discusses recommendations from autistic authors and recommendations from my data analysis of these stories, identifies limitations of this study and future research suggestions, and concludes with a call to action.

Research Questions and Interpretation of Findings

The central research question guiding my research was: What are the lived experiences of autistic adults? As I cultivated my research, I developed more specific research questions:

1. What did Adam's story tell us about:
   a. The lives of autistic people?
   b. Societal and structural responses to autism?

Adam's story reflected the diverse experiences of autistic adults and needs that are rarely met by society. Through his story, it quickly became clear needs are too often not met because they are not adequately understood. Adam's story also countered many stereotypes about autism; he very much desired relationships, felt isolated and lonely without friends, and despite successfully working 40 hours a week, has had to cope with enormous challenges to get to this point. His story highlighted issues of society responding to neurological differences by labeling these differences as deficits.

2. How do experiences described in autobiographical literature by autistic adults support, refute, exemplify, or amplify Adam's experiences?

Although specific experiences varied, thematic categories stemming from Adam's story were similar to ones also noted in the autobiographies. The similarity of themes despite vast differences of experience suggested the experiences of autistic adults can be examined in the realm of a neurotype. Though there is a whole spectrum of neurodivergent experiences autistic adults experience, their experiences are more similar to each other than they are to different neurotypes (such as neurotypical experiences). When coding from Adam's story was combined with the autobiographical constant comparison model, the following categories and subcategories emerged:

A. Isolation
   a. Mental Health
   b. Societal Expectations
   c. Medical Treatment and Diagnosis
B. Influence of Parents
C. Differences in Needs: Examples from Education and Employment
D. Empowerment
   a. Understanding One's Own Behavior Through ASD Diagnosis
      i. Sensory Experiences
E. Relationships
   a. Friendships
   b. Romantic Relationships
   c. Parenting

Isolation (Mental Health, Societal Expectations, Medical Treatment and Diagnosis)

Isolation occurred in a number of settings, including psychiatric hospitals, institutions, school, homes, places of employment, and sometimes in a marriage or friendship. Situations often leading to isolation included rejection from peers or romantic partners, being victims of bullying, not being given explanation for social rejection, societal expectations being forced on autistic people, exclusion from treatment planning, and misdiagnosis. These situations emerged via exchanges between autistic people and service providers, medical personnel, teachers, parents, friends, and partners. The exchanges were usually one sided in that the autistic person did not have much of a say in how an event played out, or they were rejected without being told why. As a result of these interactions, many authors, including Adam, experienced mental health issues, feelings of shame from not being able to fit in, feeling misunderstood by society, resentment toward parents or peers, and feeling as though they lived in their own worlds because their differences were not accepted by society. Mental Health, Societal Expectations, and Medical Treatment and Diagnosis were listed as subcategories for Isolation because they closely intertwined with experiences of Isolation.

Influence of Parents

Regardless of whether the impact parents made on their autistic children was helpful or challenging, the impact itself was often profound and had lasting consequences throughout their children's lives. Though some parents did not understand their child's differences, other parents tried to learn everything they could about autism and related support. Interactions causing the most stress between parents and children included punishments without explanation as to what their child was doing wrong or how they could behave differently. On the other hand, although some autistic people felt dismissed by society as a whole, they recognized their parents saw their full potential and believed in them, thereby helping them succeed. As a result of the influence of their parents, authors felt dismissed and misunderstood with feelings of resentment toward their parents, or they felt supported and appreciated their parents' involvement and advocacy.

Differences in Needs: Examples From Education and Employment

The authors' experiences were reflected in different supports pertaining to diverse needs at their places of employment or schools, ranging from preschool through college. Several authors described situations in the classroom in which their teachers punished them for not understanding the material or for behaving differently than other students. When they grew older, employers often fired them, not because of poor work, but because their social interactions were different from their colleagues. Conversely, some students thrived because they were encouraged by specific teachers to follow their special interests and passions, and some adults thrived in their workplaces with the right supports and mentors. Many autistic authors seemed to be punished for not conforming to societal norms rather than evaluated on the actual quality of work they produced. Others, who had supportive teachers and employers who understood their strengths and passions and included them in conversations related to their needs, were able to find or create the right environment in which they could thrive.

Empowerment (Understanding Behavior via ASD Diagnosis, Sensory Experiences)

For many authors, empowerment came from understanding their diverse needs through the context of their ASD diagnosis, including their sensory needs and how these specific needs affected daily interactions and experiences. Certain authors were able to express themselves and their experiences through writing, poetry, or music, and feel a sense of catharsis. For many, being able to communicate their experiences with loved ones, especially after receiving their ASD diagnosis, led to understanding and acceptance. Though specific experiences leading to feelings of empowerment varied greatly for each author, a common pattern in this theme was all actions led to feelings of pride, accomplishment, acceptance, and personal autonomy.

Relationships (Friendships, Romantic Relationships, Parenting)

Several authors yearned for friendship but were shunned by their peers without explanation. Others created close contacts with peers and felt supported and loved. Regardless of what type of relationship was described, at some point in their relationships, most authors came to understand they engaged with the world and their peers differently and had to figure out what that meant for their relationships. Outcomes of these relationships differed greatly from author to author, but the described relationships had profound impact on the authors' happiness, support, and sense of belonging.

Recommendations From Autistic Authors

It is important to note there is much diversity within the neurotype of autism, and many different needs. Erevelles and Minear (2010) reiterated disability is not a biological category of deficits and pathology, but simply another component of one's identity. According to the theory of intersectionality, race, gender, sexual orientation, class, and disability are not separate components of a person's identity; rather, these components influence each other and the construct of a person's identity as a whole. The authors' demographic data are presented in Table 4. A person's life experiences are intertwined with different facets of their personality. By taking into account these factors of a person's identity, we can begin to see disability is often more influenced by social and cultural constructs of what is "abnormal" and less influenced by the actual "pathology" of the individual (Erevelles & Minear, 2010; Liasidou, 2012).

The intersectionality of gender, sexuality, and disability has not been researched in much depth, but the research that does exist reflects an axis of social difference that may be related in that they counter the dominant social normalities of expression (Barnett, 2017). Countering the dominant social normalities of expression leads to negative attitudes toward people with disabilities, and these negative attitudes are perpetuated by attitudes toward other factors such as gender and sexuality (Barnett, 2017). Liasidou (2012) contended when adding factors such as race, ethnicity, gender, and socioeconomic background, students with disabilities face multiple oppressions, or what can be referred to as intersectional subordination. Understanding a student's experience based on the intersectionality of multiple factors is necessary to create appropriate and effective support plans (Barnett, 2017; Liasidou, 2012). Rather than focusing on individual pathology of students with disabilities, it is necessary to recognize how schools and social contexts perpetuate and increase barriers for people with disabilities (Liasidou, 2012).

Furthermore, research has shown students placed in what Liasidou (2012) referred to as "controversial categories of pathology" (p. 173) are typically those who come from minority backgrounds and lower socioeconomic standing. Consequentially, these students are often placed in separate special education settings with overcrowded classrooms and inadequate teacher training. A future study can elaborate on the diverse needs within the autism community, and the impact of intersectionality on each individual's needs.

Table 4. Demographic Information

Author	Book Title	a. Age of Author When Writing b. Age at Diagnosis c. Time Period Written About	Demographic Information Provided (e.g., gender, race/ethnicity, sexual orientation)
Adam			
1. Jen Birch (2003)	*Congratulations! It's Asperger Syndrome*	a. 46 b. 43 c. Mostly adulthood but also some childhood and adolescence	– Identifies as non-binary – Born and raised in New Zealand
2. Lucy Blackman (1999)	*Lucy's Story: Autism and Other Adventures*	a. early 20s b. 6 c. Lifetime up until her early 20s	– Female – Born and raised in Australia
3. Samantha Craft (2018)	*Everyday Aspergers*	a. adult b. adult; Asperger Syndrome, Dyslexia, Dyspraxia c. childhood to midlife	– Female
4. Dominique Dumortier (2002)	*From Another Planet: Autism From Within*	a. young adult b. around 24 years c. Mostly adulthood reflections, with some childhood reflections	– Female – Takes place in Belgium

(*Continued*)

Table 4. Continued

5. Temple Grandin and Margaret M. Scariano (1986)	*Emergence: Labeled Autistic*	a. late 30s b. 2 (considered a form of brain damage) c. Lifetime to late 30s	– Female – White
6. Alison Hale (2017)	*My World is Not Your World*	a. Part 1 of book: 26 years old, and wrote it before she was diagnosed with ASD b. ASD and Dyslexia; diagnosed with ASD in 1996 c. Discusses a lot about schooling and her difficulties with dyslexia as well as ASD	– Female – Born and raised in England
7. Kenneth Hall (2001)	*Asperger Syndrome, the Universe and Everything*	a. 10 b. 8 c. Childhood; has a chapter dedicated to his strengths	– Male – Lives in Northern Ireland
8. Dawn Prince-Hughes (2004)	*Songs of the Gorilla Nation*	a. 30s–40s b. 36; Asperger Syndrome c. Lifetime up until her early 20s	– Grew up in America – Identified as gay
9. Luke Jackson (2002)	*Freaks, Geeks & Asperger Syndrome: A User Guide to Adolescence*	a. 13 b. 7, but found out at age 12 (Asperger Syndrome and Dyspraxic) c. Mostly adolescence. Combined stories about childhood and adolescence with advice for other adolescents, parents, and therapists	– Male
10. Nita Jackson (2002)	*Standing Down Falling Up: Asperger's Syndrome from the Inside Out*	a. current age was 18, not sure of age when writing b. Asperger Syndrome, Bipolar Disorder, Dyslexic, Underactive Thyroid, Dyspraxic c. Childhood and adolescent experiences	– Female – Lived near London

11. Laura James (2017)	*Odd Girl Out: An Autistic Woman in a Neurotypical World*	a. 40s b. 40s: Asperger Syndrome; Ehlers-Danlos Syndrome; Postural Orthostatic Tachycardia Syndrome c. Mostly adulthood, marriage, and parenting. Self-discovery through ASD diagnosis	–	Female Lives in Norfolk, England
12. Cynthia Kim (2015)	*Nerdy, Shy, and Socially Inappropriate: A User Guide to an Asperger Life*	a. Set during 40s or 50s b. Diagnosed in 40s, Asperger Syndrome; married with one adult daughter and self-employed c. Throughout life	–	Female
13. Wendy Lawson (1998)	*Life Behind Glass: A Personal Account of Autism Spectrum Disorder.*	a. "I began to write it (this book) over 20 years ago. However, I believe that it could not have been written before now because we were not ready to receive its message" (p. ii) b. 42 c. Chapters broken into themes in chronological order of life	–	Female
14. Thomas A. McKean (1994)	*Soon Will Come the Light: A View From Inside the Autism Puzzle*	a. 26 b. 14	–	Male

(Continued)

Table 4. Continued

15. Tito Rajarshi Mukhopadhyay (2000)	Beyond the Silence: My Life, the World, and Autism.	a. 8 and 11 c. His life thus far. Wrote his story as the story of a young boy, rather than in the 1st person. Enjoyed writing prose and poetry	– Male – Born and raised in India
16. Edgar Schneider (1999)	Discovering my Autism	a. adult b. in his 40s (ADD and HFA) "I am part of a group called HFA. Those of us with normal communication capabilities are said to have AS. What we all share, of course, is emotional deficit" (p. 26) c. mostly reflections about adulthood with some memories regarding adolescence and childhood.	– Male
17. Stephen Shore (2003)	Beyond the wall: Personal experiences with Autism and Asperger Syndrome	a. young adult b. age 2; atypical development, psychotic behaviors, strong autistic tendencies c. childhood and adulthood up until current age	– Male
18. Steve Slavin (2018)	Looking for normal: Autism and other complicated stuff.	a. 50s b. 48 in 2008 c. Life until this point	– Male – Born and raised in West London

19. Liane Holliday Willey (1999)	*Pretending to be Normal: Living with Asperger's Syndrome*	a. adult b. 38? Diagnosed with AS after her daughter was diagnosed with AS. "Though it has taken 38 years, I cannot express what a relief I feel to finally 'get' me!" (p. 18) c. Lifetime. Begins each chapter with a poem, communication through poetry like many other authors	– Female
20. Donna Williams (1992)	*Nobody Nowhere: The Remarkable Autobiography of an Autistic Girl.*	c. Lifetime/wrote in passages rather than chapters	– Female

To emphasize valuable insider perspective encouraged by the social model of disability, Table 5 presents quotes directly from the 20 autobiography authors. These quotes can be used to advise therapists, medical professionals, parents, family members, and society about autism.

These quotes are reflective of neurotypical privilege in that those with disabilities are often not part of collaboration, even for their own services (Martin, 2020). A simple solution would be to collaborate with autistic people to create inclusive workplaces and universities that support, encourage, and accept everyone's diverse talents and needs. Collaboration across disciplines and across neurodiversity, listening with open minds, and learning and growing together will provide equitable services. These quotes also reflect themes discussed in Chapter Seven, highlighting diverse needs of each autistic person.

Table 5. Advice from Autistics About Autism

"As a rule therapists object to catering to fixations. But many fixations in autistic-type children have to do with a need for reducing arousal in an overactive nervous system. By concentrating on the fixation, they block out other stimulation which they cannot handle. Repetitive, monotonous stimulation may reduce neural firing in normal adults" (Grandin & Scariano, 1986, p. 105).

"ABA is something which helped me a lot…I have done really well with ABA…I would definitely recommend ABA for any kid. For a start kids are not punished. They are encouraged instead…I help Mum with ABA ideas a lot…We always have a discussion if there are going to be any rule changes. Sometimes I give her ideas for fairer rules. Sometimes when I make up a rule which makes things more difficult for me she says she is glad I am a very honest boy" (Hall, 2001, pp. 67–68).

"A special interest has magical powers. It can compel an unruly child to behave when it is used as a reward. It can help an Aspie find friends among others who enjoy the same interest. It can simultaneously satisfy the need for inquiry and calm…can be the ticket to happy employment" (Holliday, 1999, p. 133).

Table 5. Continued

"To their credit, my parents never hid from me the fact I was different from other children. The word "autism" was mentioned as if it were any other word. I feel that it is important for parents to disclose to their children their differences as soon as practical...A good addition to such a discussion might be to explore how certain weaknesses are worked with or accommodated...Early disclosures of differences can avoid identity crises later in life when the challenges of being on the autism spectrum become more apparent and almost force the issue of disclosure. The other side of the coin is that finding out about one's autism spectrum diagnosis later in life engenders a great sense of relief and better self-awareness" (Shore, 2003, p. 58).

"I have noticed that I tend to not agree with the ideals and philosophies of many of the professionals in the autism field. They must have an understanding of the definition of autism. This does not mean that they have the DSM diagnostic criteria memorized. What is listed does not even scratch the surface of what autism is. No, they must have an understanding that goes deeper than that. They must be aware of the sensory problems, they must have knowledge on how they are treated and how they may be treated in the future. They must understand the subtle reasons for the lack of communication skills, and have an understanding of the intense fear that people with autism often experience I want people who are willing to look at a person with autism and see a person." (McKean, 1994, p. 61)

"Lived experience is the true teller of how it is ... People can help one another, yes; but helping depends firstly upon not assuming that we know what the other person's life is life; the first step is to acknowledge that we do not know, but that we can listen, observe, share and (up to a point) learn. The "Insider Knowledge," though, remains the domain of the individual who has lived it" (Birch, 2003, p. 43).

"Recently I explained to my husband that I was confused by most of mankind's behavior and that I felt alone and isolated. During our conversation several things occurred to me. I was reminded that people frequently judge and categorize other people, and that I tend to think differently than the average person. I also realized the following: I pick up on others' energies and emotions; I still long to belong and be seen; some people seem less aware of self than me; just because some claim they adhere to certain principles doesn't mean they do; and people lump collective thoughts into a theory and then generalize about a set of people" (Craft, 2018, p. 341).

(Continued)

Table 5. Continued

"My way of operating is not wrong, but different, since it relates to my physical environment as I experience it. My way of compensating bridges the gap between 'my world' and 'the world.' My compensations are physiological and psychological devices for coping and are avital part of my survival" (Alison Hale, 2017, p. 125).

"Kids who are different should not have to do things which are pointless just to be the same as other kids. For example some kids with autism don't like to speak. That is because they don't see the point in it. That's just the way I feel about handwriting. So they shouldn't be forced to speak if they don't want to" (Hall, 2001, p. 100).

"It is hard to blame her when the cut-and-dried description provided by the DSM-IV makes people with Asperger's seem to be the epitome of cold disinterest, complete uncaring, and total self-absorption. What Tara learned, and what I hasten to remind the reader, is that the characteristics described in the DSM-IV are just that: they are descriptions of coping behaviors and not descriptions, necessarily, of innate orientation. People with Asperger's seem not to want to reach out, but it is not always a problem of desire, but one of comfort: they need to feel at ease in their bodies and at ease with people they might be interested in knowing ... Wanting to demonstrate to myself as much as to Tara that I didn't have to live as a diagnostic description, I laid out my plan of action" (Prince-Hughes, 2004, p. 175)

"Adults seem to make a really big deal of getting people to look at them when they are talking. Apparently it is seen as rude if you don't look at least in the direction of the speaker. This world is full of so many stupid rules! I really hate this one ... When I look someone straight in the eye, particularly someone I am not familiar with, the feeling is so uncomfortable that I cannot really describe it ... whilst someone is talking I find myself staring really hard and looking at their features and completely forgetting to listen to what they are saying" (Luke Jackson, 2002, p. 71)

"As a result of growing up undiagnosed, I've developed a lot of instinctive coping strategies for dealing with the challenges of autism. One of the easiest was a strong reliance on rules, routines, and pattern recognition. In fact, many of the traits that psychologists label rigid and routine behaviors actually feel like coping strategies for me. Adherence to routines. Resistance to change. Reliance on social scripts.
Attachment to rules" (Kim, 2015, p. 86).

"By understanding the hopes, dreams, strengths and weaknesses of autistic people, society can gain a deeper and rounder view of human nature" (Lawson, 1998, p. ii).

Table 5. Continued

"One day I dream that we can grow in a matured society where nobody would be 'normal or abnormal' but just human beings, accepting any other human being – ready to grow together" (Mukhopadhyay, 2000, p. 58).

"Alternatively, can we not just accept that some people are a differently shaped peg to the hole that society has designed for them? I'm sure those clever scientists have my best interests at heart- and, of course, all of that research funding in their bank accounts. But even if there were a cure for autism, how exactly would it work?" (Slavin, 2018, p. 309)

"It was hard to be A-okay with AS when society was still pretty darn unaccepting. Pretending to be Normal was my first step toward proclaiming autistic equality was a right not a privilege" (Willey, p. 135).

"What I do want to accomplish with this story is to tell some of what other people with autism have experienced, and much of what I have experienced as a person with autism we autistics are building an emergent culture. We individuals, with our cultures of one, are building a culture of many" (Prince-Hughes, 2004, p. 7).

"Autistic people bring so much to the world...we are human with the same hopes and fears and dreams and desires as everyone else. Instead of an endless search for a cause, many autistic people feel – rightly, I believe – that money should be spent on finding ways to support children and adults on the spectrum. Education and employment should be made more accessible and inclusive" (James, 2017, p. 145).

"It wasn't until I discovered the social model of disability that I was able to make my peace with the "disabled" label. The traditional model of disability- the medical model- looks at a disabled person's body as something that is broken and needs to be fixed. The social model points to the way society is organized as the limiting factor for disabled people. Removing barriers like negative attitudes toward disabled people and a lack of supports and adaptations are the focus of the social model. So yes, I am disabled. Many of my autistic traits make life harder for me that it is for the average person. But in thinking about how my life is different because of ASD, I've also realized that some of my autistic traits are double-edged swords, simultaneously gifting me with strengths and challenges" (Kim, 2015, p. 210).

"Communication with autistic people is difficult It is my belief, however, that we just operate on a different level of communication and that once this is discovered, strategies for mutual understanding can be developed. I find the written word much easier to comprehend than the spoken word" (Lawson, 1998, p. 9).

(Continued)

Table 5. Continued

"A hope for a concrete dream of this book to reach those who would like to understand us through me. If this book is able to light even one little flame, I would be able to see my dream take its shape...It pains when people avoid us and the schools refuse to take us. I faced it and felt that every day there may be others like me who are facing the social rejection like me" (Mukhopadhyay, 2000, p. 57).

"The nifty insights and abilities that have come as a result of having Asperger's Syndrome, are the very ingredients that help to make Aspies fabulous and notable...I can't see a future without Aspies' contributions and wisdom. And for that, I am thankful" (Willey, 1999, p. 136)

So What?

When professionals are able to communicate in a way that resonates with experiences of autistic people, autistic individuals can then understand their experiences through a lens of valid management strategy, rather than a list of problem behaviors to be fixed. Jackson-Perry et al. (2020) explained therapists, doctors, and researchers should play the role of autistic allies:

> The willingness of professionals to question and overcome deficit-based approaches, rethinking their theoretical knowledge in the light of their clients' autistic subjectivity, can be a powerful tool. Rather than the imposition of deficit, this brings an acknowledgement of difficulty while recognizing the validity of autistic ways of working with those difficulties. (p. 138)

With this research, Adam and I provided an insider's perspective to autistic life experiences. The next step is to understand how researchers, therapists, and medical professionals can use this information to better inform practice. Martin (2020) stated,

> Practical scholarship that places the question "so what?" at the centre of the enquiry, has the potential to make a difference to people's lives. This will only happen if the stage beyond "so what?" is enacted so that recommendations

are translated into an action and evaluation cycle that ultimately underpins sustainable change. Inclusion and insider perspectives need to inform practical research in order for a sufficiently rounded picture to emerge. (p. 152)

Recommendations for teachers, researchers, medical professionals, parents and families, and society in general are presented next:

Researchers

- Whenever possible, collaborate with autistic researchers.
- Qualitative data is just as important and relevant as quantitative data.
- Understanding why neurodivergent behaviors occur is more important than labeling behaviors as a deficit.
- Centralize voices of the people you are researching—in this case, autistic adults.
- Disseminate your research in ways accessible to a majority (e.g., books, blog posts, free articles, videos).

Teachers, Therapists, Psychologists, and Psychiatrists

- A special interest, or what is referred to as a fixation or obsession in medical terms, can be used to everyone's advantage. By using the autistic person's special interest, teachers and practitioners can engage the student in a meaningful way. Special interests can also be used as rewards to motivate students to engage in an activity. Conversely, special interests should not be taken away as a punishment, because doing so will lower motivation to succeed.
- Whenever possible, include the client or student in treatment planning.
- Autism is more than the diagnostic criteria listed in the DSM. To truly understand their needs, listen to the diverse experiences of each autistic client or student.
- Do not impose neurotypical expectations and activities on neurodivergent individuals.

Everyone has their own set of strengths and challenges, and it is imperative to get to know your neurodivergent clients and students and work on needs they desire, not which are imposed on them.

Parents and Families

- Whenever possible, talk with your child, rather than about your child. Include your autistic child as much as you can in treatment planning. Let them share concerns and experiences with doctors, therapists, and teachers.
- Share your child's ASD diagnosis with them at the earliest appropriate time. Many authors relayed their diagnosis helped them understand themselves better.
- Discuss your child's specific strengths and challenges related to ASD and how you can support them. Ask them if and how they feel different from their peers and how you can support them.

General Society

- If you are confused by somebody's behavior, assume they are just as confused by your behavior.
- It is not the neurodivergent person's responsibility to conform to neurotypical societal norms. There is a mutual lack of understanding between neurotypical and neurodivergent behaviors, and both must strive to understand each other.
- Understanding an autistic person's special interest is a great way to engage with an autistic person. Remember, just because they might be speaking a lot about one topic does not mean they are not interested in you or your topics of interests; rather, their monotropic attention tunnel allows them the capacity to focus on one emotionally charged topic at a time.
- Assume stereotypes you have about autism are not accurate.

Board Certified Behavior Analysts

While most of the authors did not directly discuss the field of Applied Behavior Analysis (ABA), the science and intervention of ABA is one of the most used, and most scientifically supported, approach to support autistic people (Veneziano & Shea, 2022). Thus, it is imperative to discuss how the concepts of the neurodiversity paradigm and monotropism theory can be applied to improve the practices of ABA. In addition to the previous sections, behavior analysts can:

- Engage in cross-disciplinary collaboration: Recognize that ABA is not the ONLY support that can help autistic people.
- Community engagement: Respectfully share the recommendations with other service providers (General Society; Parents & Families; Teachers, Therapists, Psychologists, & Psychiatrists; Researchers).
- Center your clients' voice: Involve your clients in treatment planning and progress monitoring (what do **they** want to work on; which strategies/approaches feel best to **them**)
- Self-Reflection: Why are you choosing that particular goal/intervention? Is it for your client's benefit or the comfort of neurotypicals in alignment with socio-cultural & behavioral expectations?
  - Who decides what are "socially significant behaviors"
- View your role as co-collaborators: You are an expert in behavior; your client is the expert in Autism Spectrum Disorder.
- Utilize nontraditional research: blogs/social media pages/books written by neurodiverse authors to better understand a variety of lived experiences and needs.
- Emphasize intersectionality: Autism is just one part of a person's identity. Ensure that other factors are being taken into consideration during treatment planning (ethnicity, gender identity, culture, race, class, physical ability, immigration/refugee experiences, language, education, etc.).
- Dissemination of information: Behavior Analytic Journals and Conferences should recruit autistic voices and whenever possible, compensate autistic individuals for taking the time our of

their personal lives to share their lived experiences, which in turn helps behavior analysts improve our professional practices.
- Understand, teach, and apply the concept of the Double Empathy Problem: support your clients while educating ourselves, our field, and society on how to create more inclusive communities.

Limitations of Study

As with any research study, there were limitations of this study. First, gathering one person's story and reading 20 autobiographies results in a small sample size and is therefore not fully reflective of the many autistic adults in the world today. As of 2019, it was estimated one out of every 270 people has autism (Global Burden of Diseases, 2020). Although these themes serve as a starting point to understanding neurodivergence, autism falls across an expansive spectrum and themes are not generalizable to the entire autistic population. Furthermore, these authors were able to articulate their words in stories, whereas some autistic individuals are not able to articulate their experiences in this way. Additionally, only autistic authors who were privileged enough to have the opportunity for their books to be published are reflected in this sample. While a limited sample size is common in research using autobiographical accounts of marginalized communities, the limited first-person autistic accounts to be published thus far outweigh the limitation of the sample size. The themes reflected in this research were meant to encourage researchers, parents, therapists, teachers, and society to view neurodiversity as differences in experiencing the world, rather than behavioral deficits, but it should be noted that the experiences of autistic people can vary greatly.

Another limitation discussed in detail in Chapter Two involved the researcher as a research instrument. Thus, my professional training and personal beliefs in some way impacted analysis of Adam's story and the autobiographies. Though there is no solution to this ethical dilemma, it is important to acknowledge it and recognize the alternative would mean not having a platform for Adam and the other 20 autistic authors to have their voices be centered in the conversation.

Future Research

This study provides a starting point for understanding autistic experiences in the neurodiversity paradigm. Future research topics include the following:

- Though Adam's story did not indicate any sexual abuse, several autobiographies described instances of sexual abuse, nonconsensual sexual encounters, and abusive relationships. Future research should explore the prevalence of autistic authors being victimized in this way and determine how we can prevent this from happening in the future.
- Another emergent topic from the autobiographies, which Adam's story did not cover, came from female authors who asserted the need for better diagnostic criteria and understanding of how autism manifests differently in women. The current DSM criteria focuses on how autism manifests in boys and men, whose behaviors often differ from autistic women. Women more easily mimic social behaviors, thus frequently resulting in misdiagnosis and limited access to supports they need.
- To expand on the current study, inclusion criteria could be increased to allow for more autobiographies to be read and analyzed. Including a greater variety of autobiographies would allow for a more in-depth analysis into different cultural backgrounds and the impact of cultural understanding of autism on success or access to support for autistic individuals.
- As discussed in a previous section, there are diverse needs within the autism community, and the impact of intersectionality each individual's needs should be studied in detail to gain a more complete understanding of autistic experiences.

- Future research should also analyze more informal content created by autistic adults (e.g., blog posts, social media posts, YouTube videos, poetry, music, and songs).

Significance of Study

The majority of autism-related research has focused on causes of autism, rather than life experiences and needs of autistic people (Roberston, 2010). Additionally, previous autism- related research has not focused on autistic adult-related needs. Or, as Slavin (2018) said in his book when he was trying to gain information about ASD after his diagnosis:

> My initial internet searches revealed a distinct lack of information relating to the more mature person on the spectrum. In fact, the casual observer could have easily concluded that autistic children become neurotypical the moment they pass their eighteenth birthday. This, as we know, is untrue. So why exactly wasn't anyone talking about the problems older autistic's face in the workplace, in their relationships, and with their mental health? Where could I read about stuff that related to me? . . . So in 2010, I launched the self-help website adultswithautism.org.uk ...It was clear that most autistic adults felt isolated, marginalised, and helpless. (pp. 298–299)

In their stories, many autistic authors communicated experiences not previously addressed. They were able to create a window into how they understood the world and how societal understandings of autism affected their daily lives. By including voices of autistic individuals, I honored my commitment to represent these individuals as experts in their own lives, navigating their experiences, hopes, fears, and desires to create future supports with them rather than for them. Importantly, I recognize each individual has their own unique experiences, but reemphasize there were significant commonalities within neurotypes. This research integrated Adam's story in a relatable, accessible way by analyzing emergent themes from several additional stories.

Call to Action

Only someone who is autistic can be considered an expert in their experiences of autism. It is imperative, as researchers and clinicians, we recognize our roles as ones of support rather than ones of authority to best serve the needs of our clients. We can start by simply listening directly to our clients to better understand their experiences and subsequent needs. We can advocate alongside them for services they desire in a way most beneficial to them. Researchers can continue to fill the void in research related to autistic adult's experiences and needs by centering the voices of autistic adults. Clinicians can expand their understanding of autism from the DSM criteria to the lived experiences of their autistic clients. Finally, to create an equitable future for autistic adults, society needs to recognize it is as much our responsibility to understand neurodivergent needs as it is for neurodivergent individuals to understand neurotypical behaviors.

References

American Psychiatric Association. (1980). *Diagnostic and statistical manual of mental disorders* (3rd ed.). American Psychiatric Publishing.

American Psychiatric Association. (1994). *Diagnostic and statistical manual of mental disorders* (4th ed.). American Psychiatric Publishing.

American Psychiatric Association. (2013). *Diagnostic and statistical manual of mental disorders* (5th ed.). American Psychiatric Publishing.

Anderson, G. L., & Herr, K. (1999). The new paradigm wars: Is there room for rigorous practitioner knowledge in schools and universities? *Educational Researcher, 28*(5), 12–21. https://doi.org/10.3102/0013189X028005012

Angulo-Jimenez, H., & DeThorne, L. (2019). Narratives about autism: An analysis of YouTube videos by individuals who self-identify as autistic. *American Journal of Speech-Language Pathology, 28*(2), 569–590. https://doi.org/10.1044/2018-AJSLP-18-0045

Arnett, J. J. (2000). Emerging adulthood: A theory of development from the late teens through the twenties. *American Psychologist, 55*(5), 469–480. https://doi.org/10.1037/0003-066X.55.5.469

Ashby, C. E., & Causton-Theoharis, J. N. (2009). Disqualified in the human race: A close reading of the autobiographies of individuals identified as autistic. *International Journal of Inclusive Education, 13*(5), 501–516. https://doi.org/10.1080/13603110801886673

Autistic Self-Advocacy Network. (2016). *Nothing about us without us.* https://autisticadvocacy.org/home

Baglieri, S., Valle, J. W., Connor, D. J., & Gallagher, D. J. (2011). Disability studies in education: The need for a plurality of perspectives on disability. *Remedial and Special Education, 32*(4), 267–278. https://doi.org/10.1177/0741932510362200

Barnett, J. P. (2017). Intersectional harassment and deviant embodiment among Autistic adults: (dis)ability, gender and sexuality. *Culture, Health & Sexuality, 19*(11), 1210–1224. https://doi.org/10.1080/13691058.2017.1309070

Birch, J. (2003). *Congratulations! It's Asperger syndrome.* Jessica Kingsley Publishers.

Bishop, R. (2005). Freeing ourselves from neocolonial domination in research: A Kaupapa Maori approach to creating knowledge. In N. K. Denzin & Y. S. Lincoln (Eds.), *The SAGE handbook of qualitative research* (3rd ed., pp. 109–138). SAGE Publications.

Blackman, L. (1999). *Lucy's story: Autism and other adventures.* Jessica Kingsley Publishers.

Caine, V., Steeves, P., Clandinin, D. J., Estefan, A., Huber, J., & Murphy, M. S. (2018). Social justice practice: A narrative inquiry perspective. *Education, Citizenship & Social Justice, 13*(2), 133–143. https://doi.org/10.1177/1746197917710235

Chapman, R. (2020). Defining neurodiversity for research and practice. In H. B. Rosqvist, N. Chown, & A. Stenning (Eds.), *Neurodiversity studies: A new critical paradigm* (pp. 218–220). Routledge.

Charlton, J. (1998). *Nothing about us without us: Disability oppression and empowerment.* University of California Press.

Charmaz, K. (2012). *Constructing grounded theory* (2nd ed.). SAGE Publications.

Chase, S. (2012) Narrative inquiry: Still a field in the making. In N. K. Denzin & Y. S. Lincoln (Eds.), *Collecting and interpreting qualitative materials* (4th ed., pp. 55–85). SAGE Publications.

Chown, N. (2020). Language games used to construct autism as pathology. In H. B. Rosqvist, N. Chown, & A. Stenning (Eds.), *Neurodiversity studies: A new critical paradigm* (pp. 27–38). Routledge.

Clandinin, D. J., Cave, M. T., & Berendonk, C. (2017). Narrative inquiry: A relational research methodology for medical education. *Medical Education, 51*(1), 89–96. https://doi.org/10.1111/medu.13136

Clandinin, D. J., & Connelly, F. M. (2000). *Narrative inquiry: Experience and story in qualitative research.* Jossey-Bass.

Cook, K. A., & Willmerdinger, A. N. (2015). *The history of autism* [Narrative document]. Furman University Scholar Exchange. http://scholarexchange.furman.edu/schopler-about/1

Couser, T. (2004). *Vulnerable subjects, ethics and life writing.* Cornell University Press.

Craft, S. (2018). *Everyday Aspergers.* Your Stories Matter.

Creswell, J. W., & Poth, C. N. (2018) *Qualitative inquiry and research designs* (4th ed.). SAGE Publications.

DePape, A.-M., & Lindsay, S. (2016). Lived experiences from the perspective of individuals with Autism Spectrum Disorder: A qualitative meta-synthesis. *Focus on

Autism and Other Developmental Disabilities, 31(1), 60–71. https://doi.org/10.1177/1088357615587504

Dumortier, D. (2002). *From another planet: Autism from within.* Lucky Duck Publishing.

Elias, R., & White, S. W. (2018). Autism goes to college: Understanding the needs of a student population on the rise. *Journal of Autism and Developmental Disorders, 48,* 732–746. https://doi.org/10.1007/s10803-017-3075-7

Erevelles, N., & Minear, A. (2010). Unspeakable offenses: Untangling race and disability in discourses of intersectionality. *Journal of Literary & Cultural Disability Studies, 4*(2), 127–145. https://doi.org/10.3828/jlcds.2010.11

Fenstein, A. (2010). *A history of autism: Conversations with the pioneers.* Wiley-Blackwell.

Ferguson, D. L., & Ferguson, P. M. (2000). Qualitative research in special education: Notes toward an open inquiry instead of a new orthodoxy? *Journal of the Association for Persons with Severe Handicaps, 25*(3), 180–185. https://doi.org/10.2511/rpsd.25.3.180

Ferri, B. A. (2011). Disability life writing and the politics of knowing. *Teachers College Record, 113*(10), 2267–2282. https://www.tcrecord.org/Content.asp?ContentId=16433

First, J. M., Cheak-Zamora, N. C., Teti, M., Maurer-Batjer, A., & L First, N. (2019). Youth perceptions of stress and coping when transitioning to adulthood with autism: A photovoice study. *Qualitative Social Work, 18*(4), 601–620. https://doi.org/10.1177/1473325018757078

GBD 2019 Diseases and Injuries Collaborators. (2020). Global burden of 369 diseases and injuries in 204 countries and territories, 1990–2019: A systematic analysis for the Global Burden of Disease Study 2019. *The Lancet, 396*(10258): 1204–1222. https://doi.org/10.1016/S0140-6736(20)30925-9

Gerhardt, P. F., & Lainer, I. (2010). Addressing the needs of adolescents and adults with autism: A crisis on the horizon. *Journal of Contemporary Psychotherapy, 41,* 37–45. https://doi.org/10.1007/s10879-010-9160-2

Glaser, B., & Strauss, A. (1967). *The discovery of grounded theory.* Aldine Publishing Company. Grandin, T., & Scariano, M. M. (1986). *Emergence: Labeled autistic.* Warner Books.

Gready, P. (2013). The public life of narratives: Ethics, politics, methods. In M. Andrews, C. Squire, & M. Tamboukou (Eds.) *Doing narrative research* (2nd ed., pp. 240–254). SAGE Publications.

Grypdonck, M. H. (2006). Qualitative health research in the era of evidence-based practice. *Qualitative Health Research, 16*(10), 1371–1385. https://doi.org/10.1177/1049732306294089

Hall, K. (2001). *Asperger Syndrome, the universe and everything.* Jessica Kingsley Publishers.

Harrison, J., MacGibbon, L., & Morton, M. (2001). Regimes of trustworthiness in qualitative research: The rigors of reciprocity. *Qualitative Inquiry, 7*(3), 323–345. https://doi.org/10.1177/107780040100700305

Highlen, D. (2017). Helping students with autism spectrum disorder at the community college: What does the research say? What can you do? *Community College Journal of Research and Practice, 41*(7), 447–454. https://doi.org/10.1080/10668926.2016.1199334

Hillary, A. (2020). Neurodiversity and cross-cultural communications. In H. B. Rosqvist, N. Chown, & A. Stenning (Eds.), *Neurodiversity studies: A new critical paradigm* (pp. 91– 107). Routledge.

Hossain, M., Khan, N., Sultana, A., Ma, P., Lisako, E., McKyer, J., Ahmed, H. U., & Purohit, N. (2020). Prevalence of comorbid psychiatric disorders among people with autism spectrum disorder: An umbrella review of systematic reviews and meta-analyses. *Psychiatry Research, 287*, Article 112922. https://doi.org/10.1016/j.psychres.2020.112922

Hurlbutt, K., & Chalmers, L. (2002). Adults with autism speak out: Perceptions of their life experiences. *Focus on Autism and Other Developmental Disabilities, 17*(2), 103–111. https://doi.org/10.1177/10883576020170020501

Jaarsma, P., & Welin, S. (2012). Autism as a natural variation: Reflections on the claims of the neurodiversity movement. *Health Care Analysis, 20*(1), 20–30. https://doi.org/10.1007/s10728-011-0169-9

Jackson, L. (2002). *Freaks, geeks & Asperger Syndrome: A user guide to adolescence*. Jessica Kingsley Publishers.

Jackson, N. (2002). *Standing down falling up: Asperger's Syndrome from the inside out*. Lucky Duck Publishing.

Jackson-Perry, D., Rosqvist, H., Annable, J., & Kourti, M. (2020). Sensory strategies: Travels in normate sensory worlds. In H. B. Rosqvist, N. Chown, & A. Stenning (Eds.), *Neurodiversity studies: A new critical paradigm* (pp. 125–140). Routledge.

James, L. (2017). *Odd girl out: An autistic woman in a neurotypical world*. Bluebird Books for Life.

Jones, J. A. (2017). *The social experiences of young adults with autism as they transition from high school to college* [Doctoral dissertation, Capella University]. Dissertation Abstracts International Section A: Humanities and Social Sciences. ProQuest Dissertations Publishing.

Kanner, L. (1943). Autistic disturbances of affective contact. *Nervous Child, 2*(1), 217–250. http://mail.neurodiversity.com/library_kanner_1943.pdf

Kim, C. (2015). *Nerdy, shy, and socially inappropriate: A user guide to an Asperger life*. Jessica Kingsley Publishers.

Kirby, A. V., Dickie, V. A., & Baranek, G. T. (2015). Sensory experiences of children with autism spectrum disorder: In their own words. *Autism: The International Journal of Research and Practice, 19*(3), 316–326. https://doi.org/10.1177/1362361314520756

Langness, L. L., & Frank, G. (1986). *Lives: An anthropological approach to biography*. Chandler & Sharp Publishers.

Lawson, W. (1998). *Life behind glass: A personal account of autism spectrum disorder*. Jessica Kingsley Publishers.

Laxman, D. J., Taylor, J. L., DaWalt, L. S., Greenberg, J. S., & Mailick, M. R. (2019). Loss in services precedes high school exit for teens with autism spectrum disorder: A longitudinal study. *Autism Research, 12*(6), 911–921. https://doi.org/10.1002/aur.2113

Leong, D. S. M. (2016). *Scheherazade's sea – Autism, parallel embodiment and elemental empathy* [Unpublished doctoral dissertation]. University of New South Wales, Sydney.

Levy, A., & Perry, A. (2011). Outcomes in adolescent and adults with autism: A review of the literature. *Research in Autism Spectrum Disorder, 5*(4),1271–1282. https://doi.org/10.1016/j.rasd.2011.01.023

Liasidou, A. (2012). Inclusive education and critical pedagogy at the intersections of disability, race, gender and class. *Journal for Critical Education Policy Studies, 10*(1), 168–184.

Martin, N. (2020). Practical scholarship: Optimizing beneficial research collaborations between autistic scholars, professional service staff, and 'typical academics' in UK Universities. In H. B. Rosqvist, N. Chown, & A. Stenning (Eds.), *Neurodiversity studies: A new critical paradigm* (pp. 143–155). Routledge.

McDonough, J. T., & Revell, G. (2010). Accessing employment supports in the adult system for transitioning youth with autism spectrum disorders. *Journal of Vocational Rehabilitation, 32*(2010), 89–100. https://doi.org/10.3233/JVR-2010-0498

McKean, T. A. (1994). *Soon will come the light: A view from inside the autism puzzle* (2nd ed.). Future Horizons.

McKenzie, K., Ouellette-Kuntz, H., Binkhorn, A., & Demore, A. (2017). Out of school and into distress: Families of young adults with intellectual and developmental disabilities in transition. *Journal of Applied Research in Intellectual Disabilities, 30*(4), 774–781. https://doi.org/10.1111/jar.12264

Milton, D. E. M. (2012). On the ontological status of autism: The 'double empathy problem.' *Disability & Society, 27*(6), 883–887. https://doi.org/10.1080/09687599.2012.710008

Moss, G. (2004). Provisions of trustworthiness in critical narrative research: Bridging intersubjectivity and fidelity. *The Qualitative Report, 9*(2), 359–374. https://doi.org/10.46743/2160-3715/2004.1933

Mukhopadhyay, T. R. (2000). *Beyond the silence: My life, the world, and autism*. The National Autistic Society.

Murray, D., Lesser, M., & Lawson, W. (2005). Attention, monotropism and the diagnostic criteria for autism. *Autism, 9*(2), 139–156. https://doi.org/10.1177/1362361305051398

Murray, F. (2019). Me and Monotropism. *The Psychologist, 32*, 44–49.

Nadesan, M. H. (2005). *Constructing autism: Unravelling the 'truth' and understanding the social*. Routledge.

Nicholas, D. B., Hodgetts, S., Zwaigenbaum, L., Smith, L. E., Shattuck, P., Parr, J. R., Conlon, O., Germani, T., Mitchell, W., Sacrey, L., & Stothers, M. E. (2016). Research needs and priorities for transition and employment in autism: Considerations reflected in a "special interest group" at the international meeting for autism research. *Autism Research, 10*(1), 15–24. https://doi.org/10.1002/aur.1683

Pesonen, H. V., Kontu, E. K., & Pirttimaa, R. A. (2015). Sense of belonging and life transitions for two females with autism spectrum disorder in Finland. *Journal of International Special Needs Education, 18*(2), 73–86. https://doi.org/10.9782/2159-4341-18.2.73

Prince-Hughes, D. (2004). *Songs of the gorilla nation*. Three Rivers Press.

Riessman, C. K. (2008). *Narrative methods for the human sciences*. SAGE Publications.

Robertson, S. M. (2010). Neurodiversity, quality of life, and autistic adults: Shifting research and professional focuses onto real-life challenges. *Disability Studies Quarterly, 30*(1). https://doi.org/10.18061/dsq.v30i1.1069

Rosqvist, H. B., Orulv, L., Hasselblad, S., Hansson, D., Nilsson, K., & Seng, H. (2020). Designing an autistic space for research: Exploring the impact of context, space, and sociality in autistic writing processes. In H. B. Rosqvist, N. Chown, & A. Stenning (Eds.), *Neurodiversity studies: A new critical paradigm* (pp. 156–171). Routledge.

Saldaña, J. (2016). *The coding manual for qualitative researchers*. SAGE Publications.

Schalock, R. L. (2000). Three decades of quality of life. *Focus on Autism and Other Developmental Disabilities, 15*(2), 116–127. https://doi.org/10.1177/108835760001500207

Schneider, E. (1999). *Discovering my autism*. Jessica Kingsley Publishers.

Schön, D. (1995). Knowing-in-action: The new scholarship requires a new epistemology. *Change: The Magazine of Higher Learning, 27*(6), 27–34. https://doi.org/10.1080/00091383.1995.10544673

Shore, S. M. (2003). *Beyond the wall: Personal experiences with autism and Asperger syndrome* (2nd ed.). Autism Asperger Publishing.

Siebers, T. (2011). *Disability theory*. Michigan Press.

Slavin, S. (2018). *Looking for normal: Autism and other complicated stuff*. Marshwood.

Stenning, A. (2020). Understanding empathy through a study of autistic life writing: On the importance of neurodivergent morality. In H. B. Rosqvist, N. Chown, & A. Stenning (Eds.), *Neurodiversity studies: A new critical paradigm* (pp. 108–124). Routledge.

Strand, L. R. (2017). Charting relations between intersectionality theory and the neurodiversity paradigm. *Disability Studies Quarterly, 37*(2). https://dsq-sds.org/article/view/5374/4647

Tamboukou, M., Andrews, M., & Squire, C. (2013). Introduction: What is narrative research? In M. Andrews, C. Squire, & M. Tamboukou (Eds.) *Doing narrative research* (2nd ed., pp. 1–26). SAGE Publications.

Thomas, C. (2002). Disability theory: Key ideas, issues, and thinkers. In C. Barnes, M. Oliver, & L. Barton (Eds.), *Disability studies today* (pp. 38–57). Polity Press.

Tillman, L. C. (2002). Culturally sensitive research approaches: An African-American perspective. *Educational Researcher, 31*(9), 3–12. https://doi.org/10.3102/0013189X031009003

Veneziano, J., & Shea, S. (2022). They have a voice; are we listening? *Behavior Analysis in Practice*. https://doi.org/10.1007/s40617-022-00690-z

Vogt, W. P., Vogt, E. R., Gardner, D. C., & Haeffele, L. M. (2014). *Selecting the right analyses for your data: Quantitative, qualitative, and mixed methods*. The Guilford Press.

Walker, N. (2014, September 27). *Neurodiversity: Some basic terms & definitions*. Neurocosmopolitanism. http://neurocosmopolitanism.com/neurodiversity-some-basic- terms-definitions/

Weinstein, M. C. (2001). Should physicians be gatekeepers of medical resources? *Journal of Medical Ethics, 27*(1), 268–274. https://doi.org/10.1136/jme.27.4.268

Willey, L. H. (1999). *Pretending to be normal: Living with Asperger's syndrome (Autism Spectrum Disorder)*. Jessica Kingsley Publishers.

Williams, D. (1992). *Nobody nowhere: The remarkable autobiography of an autistic girl*. Jessica Kingsley Publishers.

Woodbury-Smith, M. R., Boyd, K., & Szatmari, P. (2010). Autism spectrum disorders, schizophrenia and diagnostic confusion. *Journal of Psychiatry & Neuroscience, 35*(5), 360. https://doi.org/10.1503/jpn.100130

Xu, M. A., & Storr, G. B. (2012). Learning the concept of researcher as instrument in qualitative research. *Qualitative Report, 17*(21), 1–18. https://doi.org/10.46743/2160-3715/2012.1768

About the Authors

Sneha Kohli Mathur, Ph.D., BCBA considers herself an ally to the disability and Autism communities, and started Spectrum Success, LLC in order to support individuals on the autism spectrum, while educating neurotypicals on how to create a socially inclusive community. Sneha is a Board Certified Behavior Analyst (BCBA), has Bachelor's and Master's degrees in Psychology, and a doctorate degree in Education and Disability Studies. What makes Sneha's research, teaching, and consulting unique is her expertise in two very distinct areas, applied behavior analysis and disabilities studies. She is able to layout behaviorally supported practices within a caring social-model context. Sneha's work centers on increasing the quality of life for autistic folks and her future-focused approach allows her to help individuals build long-term success.

Sneha is currently a faculty member in the Psychology Department of the University of Southern California (USC), where she teaches Master level courses in Applied Behavior Analysis, and undergraduate courses related to Autism and Neurodiversity. Sneha is also a founding member of the Equity, Diversity, and Inclusion organization in ABA, a group that works towards social justice within the field of ABA in order to create a more inclusive platform for ABA practitioners and a more equitable future for our clients.

Adam Paul Valerius, Autistic Advocate, is a young adult who was diagnosed with Asperger Syndrome at the age of 12. Adam is smart, well spoken, and motivated to break the stereotypes related to ASD. Adam is enthusiastic, keen to learn, and very insightful as to how his Asperger Syndrome effects his struggles with employment, and he is excited for the opportunity to help others on the Autism Spectrum. Adam is currently working at a full time position, but still finds the time to advise and consult with Sneha on various projects. Adam and Sneha wrote this book together and Adam has courageously shared his life story with us.

GENERAL EDITORS: SUSAN L. GABEL & SCOT DANFORTH

The book series Disability Studies in Education is dedicated to the publication of monographs and edited volumes that integrate the perspectives, methods, and theories of disability studies with the study of issues and problems of education. The series features books that further define, elaborate upon, and extend knowledge in the field of disability studies in education. Special emphasis is given to work that poses solutions to important problems facing contemporary educational theory, policy, and practice.

To order other books in this series, please contact our Customer Service Department:

peterlang@presswarehouse.com (within the U.S.)
orders@peterlang.com (outside the U.S.)

Or browse by series:

WWW.PETERLANG.COM

www.ingramcontent.com/pod-product-compliance
Lightning Source LLC
Chambersburg PA
CBHW061711300426
44115CB00014B/2643